Phenomenological Psychology

Phenomenological Psychology

An Introduction
With a glossary of
some key Heideggerian terms

Raymond J. McCall

The University of Wisconsin Press

Published 1983

The University of Wisconsin Press
114 North Murray Street
Madison, Wisconsin 53715

The University of Wisconsin Press, Ltd.
1 Gower Street
London WC1E 6HA, England

First printing

Printed in the United States of America

For LC CIP information see the colophon

ISBN 0-299-09410-3 cloth; 0-299-09414-6 paper

For Ray Jr., Tony, Timothy, Debra, and their model, mentor, and mother, Betty

Contents

Phenomenological Psychology

Introduction

The existential analysis (*Daseinsanalyse*) of Medard Boss represents an effort to apply the ideas of the philosopher Martin Heidegger (1889–1976) to personality theory and psychotherapy. Prior to 1970, although I was aware of Medard Boss's work in psychopathology, I had read only his book on sexual deviations. The reading of his 1963 book *Psychoanalysis and Daseinsanalysis,*[1] then, came to me as a revealing and moving experience, though also a frustrating one; frustrating because the translation seemed to be so unclear and uncertain and cumbersome in style, and I could find no German edition of this work. Participating in an American Psychological Association workshop conducted by Boss in the late summer of 1971 reinforced my conviction that there was a great deal of value in the Boss-Heidegger approach of which American psychologists and psychiatrists seemed sublimely ignorant. Something, I felt, ought to be done to make its insights more accessible to interested Americans. Boss was continuing to write books in German which were destined for translation into English and I feared that these would exhibit some of the same weaknesses found in *Psychoanalysis and Daseinsanalysis.* There could be no question of my undertaking another translation myself. My never-fluent German was rusty after twenty-five years of neglect and required a couple of years of intense (if sporadic) endeavor to bring it up to minimal competence. Perhaps I could have helped a literarily oriented translator with certain philosophical, logical, and clinical terms which are difficult to render in idiomatic English, but the opportunity to work with such a person was not provided. The further I looked into the matter, in any case, the more convinced I became that current translations of Boss's writings—including several works besides *Psychoanalysis and Daseinsanalysis*—were irredeemably bad, while the standard translation of Heidegger's

1. Medard Boss, *Psychoanalysis and Daseinsanalysis,* trans. L. B. Lefebre (New York: Basic Books, 1963).

masterpiece *Sein und Zeit*[2] was totally incomprehensible to the psychiatrists and psychologists to whom I showed it. I was encouraged in this negative evaluation by Boss's expressed dissatisfaction with the existing translations of his own and Heidegger's work. I realized then that only in sustained face-to-face contact with Boss could I hope to divine the full meaning of his various applications of Heideggerian principle to questions of human motivation, psychodiagnosis, and psychotherapy, which would enable me to explore with him the best possible way of putting the Boss-Heidegger position in American English. From January to June of 1977 I had the privilege of working closely with Boss in Zurich on this project.[3]

What was in question in our discussions over this six-month period was the translation of at most fifty or sixty terms which are key words in Heidegger's system, especially those aspects of his system which Boss sees as most relevant to psychological questions and which have most frequently been translated ambiguously. All or virtually all of these terms are found in Heidegger's *Sein und Zeit,* and they are used there with a repetitiousness that borders on perseveration, their sense and reference illustrated in a variety of contexts which gives the whole work a fugue-like quality. It was this, I believe, that determined the method Boss and I used to circumscribe as far as possible the precise meaning of these terms in Heidegger. Our procedure might be described as contextual rather than literal. For each of these perhaps fifty terms an effort was made to identify the element common to the various contexts in which the term was used. We thereupon attempted to approximate in English that contextually determined meaning, relying only minimally on German-English cognates and dictionary definitions.

One example, which I shall later deal with at length, is Heideg-

2. Martin Heidegger, *Sein und Zeit,* 7th ed. (Tübingen: Max Niemeyer, 1953). English translation: *Being and Time,* trans. J. Macquarrie and E. Robinson (New York: Harper and Row, 1962).

3. For this privilege I have to thank not only Dr. Boss but Marquette University, which granted me a sabbatical leave for this purpose, and also the Applied Power Foundation, Mr. Philip G. Brumder, Chairman of the Board, for underwriting the additional expense of my sojourn in Switzerland.

ger's term *zuhanden*. This word, which in everyday German means "at hand" or "on hand," is cognate with the English "to hand" and is often accordingly translated "ready to hand." In a dozen different contexts in *Sein und Zeit* the sense of *zuhanden* can be conveyed with near-perfect adequacy by the English word "useful" without any reference to the German word *Hand* or its English cognate "hand." Yet practically no one translates *zuhanden* this simply, and everyone tries to capture the metaphorical ambience of the hand image in such expressions as "handy," or "ready to hand," even though in so doing they lose or dilute the basic meaning of "useful." The principle that we should ignore the metaphorical implications and focus on the basic-meaning-in-context does not apply as neatly to all of Heidegger's major terms as in the case of *zuhanden;* on the whole, however, we found the application of the principle both plausible and surprisingly easy. The results of this joint effort form the substance of the second part of this monograph. Though I must assume responsibility for the final form of the English translations of these terms, the task would have been impossible without Medard Boss's profound understanding of Heidegger, his assured grasp of his native German, his good working knowledge of English, and his unfailing patience and graciousness. The distinctive constellation of Boss's talents and qualifications merits appreciative attention, and I would like to tell you a little more about this remarkable man.

A vigorous and tireless seventy-nine, Boss has lived all but the first two years of his life in Zurich, the *Hauptstadt* of German-Swiss culture. Though German is his language of preference, Boss is, like a great many Swiss, at home in a number of languages and seems to have little difficulty picking up additional ones (for instance, Portuguese and Hindi) on short notice. Happily for me, his spoken English is both fluent and sophisticated.

In his career as a student and practitioner of psychiatry, Boss had the enterprise and good fortune to be in direct and sustained contact with many of the truly great figures in modern psychiatry. As a young man he traveled to Vienna to begin analysis with Freud himself. After receiving his medical degree he spent several years as assistant to Eugen Bleuler, went to London and Berlin for psychoanalytic study with Ernest Jones, Karen Horney, Otto

Fenichel, and Wilhelm Reich, and, quite naturally, also studied
with an analytic group under the direction of Carl Jung in Zurich.

His extensive psychoanalytic training, however, left Boss point-
edly dissatisfied. The view of man intrinsic to psychoanalysis
seemed forced and artificial when brought to bear on the problems
of the real people he met in his consulting practice. Introduced in
the 1940s to the ideas of Heidegger by his compatriot Ludwig
Binswanger, Boss was intrigued and fascinated. This fascination
became so great that, in spite of his having only a modest background in philosophy, Boss launched on an effort to master Heidegger's thought and to test out fully its applications to psychiatry.
As soon as World War II ended Boss sought out Heidegger and
became his disciple and close personal friend for the remaining
thirty years of Heidegger's life.

Through Boss I became convinced that Heidegger's ideas had
great applicability to certain crucial questions in contemporary
psychology and psychiatry, many of these questions substantive,
but an even greater number, I believe, methodological in nature.
With Boss's account of this applicability—for the most part supported by Heidegger himself over their many years of association
—I find myself in substantial agreement. Our differences in background and approach, however, are such as to keep this agreement
from being total. Boss is, to adopt a favorite phrase of Heidegger's, first and foremost (*zunächst und zumeist*) a physician, trained
in medicine, psychiatry, and psychoanalysis (with a late conversion to a philosophical perspective), while my own training was
first in logic and the history of philosophy, and later in empirical
and clinical psychology. A common interest in psychological
theory and the dynamics of human effort and action, and a common distaste for mechanistic reductionism as a model for the interpretation of human behavior, guarantee some consensus between
us, but I do not believe they can offset our very different convictions regarding the importance of empirical scientific method in
validating the application of philosophical principles to the concrete contingencies of human experience and function. As I understand Boss on this last matter, he remains perpetually suspicious of
scientific method as applied to any aspect of the human condition
because he sees that method as inevitably physicalistic and mech-

anistic in its implications. *De facto,* Boss is probably more often right than wrong in his suspicions, considering the models of human function preferred by those schools of psychology that pride themselves on their scientific orientation: behaviorism, Gestaltism, operationism, positivism, psychonomics, and so on. One must distinguish, however, between science as an admirable enterprise which has opened to man the understanding and control of nature to a degree undreamed of before the seventeenth century, when the systematic application of the scientific method began, and *scientism,* the philosophy which regards scientific method as the sole means of arriving at truth in any sphere of intellectual endeavor. Behaviorism and logical positivism, for example, represent a scientistic philosophy rather than a scientific theory, though their partisans work hard to obscure that important distinction. A scientific theory is not one that exalts science but one that is grounded in and supported by empirical evidence. As they stand, behaviorism and logical positivism praise scientific method unstintingly but base themselves on a curious combination of epistemology (theory of knowledge), philosophy of history (specifically, an attempt to show how the historical development of the intellect has culminated in the production of science), and social philosophy (a wistful vision of how science can be used to remake human relations), the whole about as solidly based on empirical fact as, say, the *Rubaiyat of Omar Khayyam* or the *Communist Manifesto.*

Boss may have, I fear, taken too seriously the claim of the scientistically oriented to speak for science, and consequently been less than enthusiastically receptive to anything that calls itself empirical or scientific psychology. I am not sure that Boss is fully aware of how many scientifically trained and productive psychologists in the English-speaking world are moving away from the simplicism and the reductionism of early behaviorist and psychoanalytic formulations, while retaining their faith in the validity of the scientific method in psychology. The group that identifies itself as "cognitive psychologists," many psycholinguists and social learning theorists, methodological experientialists like Koch and MacLeod, the Piagetian developmentalists, and many others are gravitating toward an ever greater appreciation of the cognitive, the purposive, the conceptually (as opposed to the emotionally) human-

istic, which would make them attentive to existential-phenomenological formulations like Boss's, provided only that these formulations are responsive to the need for empirical validation.[4] It would
be most unfortunate if Boss's reaction to the abuse of empirical
method would lessen his appreciation of why the overwhelming
majority of American psychologists believe this method to be *indispensable* for the testing of hypotheses, the grounding of inductive
generalizations, and indeed for the settlement of all, or virtually
all, disputes of fact in the behavioral, as truly as in the physical and
life, sciences. Neither the validity of Boss's highly plausible theories of motivation, diagnosis, and dream interpretation nor the
effectiveness of the various psychotherapeutic procedures he advo-
cates will find full acceptance without supportive empirical evidence such as might be provided by frequency counts, incidence
figures for various diagnostic categories, reliability measures, outcome statistics, and the like. I believe I am not being unfair in
noting that to this need Boss seems singularly unresponsive. Well
trained as he is, therefore, in psychiatry and other aspects of medicine, and deeply informed about and dedicated to phenomenology
and at least one type of existential philosophy, Boss is not schooled
in empirical psychology nor particularly appreciative of the contributions which the empirical and phenomenological approaches
can make to each other. In the first part of this monograph I will
try to show how the history of the modern effort to understand the
psychological nature of the human being makes evident the necessity for an interpenetration of these two approaches. In pursuing
this objective I will not be going over very many of the points that
Boss has already made in his translated writings, such as *Psychoanalysis and Daseinsanalysis* (1963), *The Analysis of Dreams* (1958), *I
Dreamt Last Night* (1978), and *Existential Foundations of Medicine and
Psychology* (1979), though in the second part of the monograph I
will devote some effort to the clarification of certain positions

4. Sigmund Koch, "Psychology and Emerging Conceptions of Knowledge as
Unitary," in *Behaviorism and Phenomenology: Contrasting Bases for Modern Psychology*,
ed. T. W. Wann (Chicago: University of Chicago Press, 1964), pp. 1–42; Robert
B. MacLeod, "Phenomenology: a Challenge to Experimental Psychology," in
Wann, *Behaviorism and Phenomenology*, pp. 47–74; Jean Piaget, *The Origins of Intelli-
gence in Children* (New York: International Universities Press, 1952).

which Boss has taken and which I feel have been obscured by inadequate translation. On the whole, in such areas as psychotherapy and dream interpretation, I will allow Boss to speak for himself. On the other hand, I will be especially concerned to note some ways in which Heidegger's vision of man can be a source of insights for the *empirical psychologist* in several areas of his discipline, both methodological and substantive, as well as for the clinical psychopathologist and psychotherapist to whom Boss has primarily addressed his writings.

Understanding the relevance of Heidegger's philosophy to a contemporary problem of great moment to empirical psychologists, namely, the *nature of psychological functioning* as such, depends on an appreciation of the historical context in which both this problem and Heidegger's own position on the nature of man have developed. Though it would obviously be impossible in a monograph of this sort to do justice to the history of philosophical and scientific analyses and explanations of the nature of the psychological, I will attempt in brief compass to take note of certain historical trends in these analyses and explanations, and identify a few of the individuals most influential in their development, particularly since the beginning of the seventeenth century.

Before beginning this historical overview of theories of psychological functioning, let me state what I mean by the term "psychological." In what follows, "psychological" will always refer primarily to knowing (*cognition*), motivation and emotion (*appetition*), or both. Sensing, perceiving, imagining, remembering, understanding, and reasoning thus are psychological functions because they are all forms of knowledge or cognition; while desire and aversion, joy and anger, hope and fear, interest and indifference are psychological because they pertain directly to motivation (and its correlative, emotion). *Anything* psychological, in this view, is such because it relates either to the cognitive or the appetitive-affective, to knowledge or motivation-emotion, regardless of whether the "thing" in question is physical, physiological, neural, or "purely" mental.

Psychology is sometimes defined as "the science of behavior." Is behavior then not psychological? That depends. When behavior expresses desire or intention or any other appetitive condition or when it is guided by perception or understanding or any other form of cognition, it is psychological. The secretions of the pancreas and the peristaltic contractions of gastrointestinal muscles are behavioral, but unless linked in some way with cognition or appetition, such behavior is *not* psychological. Thus when it is said that psychology studies behavior, that should not be taken as implying that every muscular twitch and glandular ooze is of psychological import or value. Indeed, characteristically *human* behavior is in significant measure governed by rational understanding and conscious purpose, and a psychology that ignores or distorts this truth can hardly do justice to human psychological functioning. It is too bad that no one has publicly attempted to draw up a comprehensive list of cognitively and appetitively modulated human activities (behavioral and of other kinds), because such a list would constitute a body of facts about the human condition no item of which any self-respecting psychology could refuse to try to explain.[5]

---

5. Though the subject is mostly tangential to the present monograph, I would be glad to correspond with anyone interested in the broad outlines of such a list.

1

The Nature of Human Psychological Functioning: Historical Background

The activities we have designated as psychological—perceiving, imagining, desiring, fearing, and so on—have been the object of philosophical interest at least since the time of the early Greek thinkers (beginning in the sixth century B.C.), though it was not until the seventeenth century that theories about these functions were much influenced by ideas derived from empirical[1] science; and it was not until the nineteenth century that an attempt was made to deal with them in a manner that could itself be called scientifically empirical.

In Europe before the seventeenth century, conceptions of human psychological functioning were dominated by philosophical and theological notions derived principally from Aristotle (384–322 B.C.), Plato (427–347 B.C.), and their Christian interpreters, St. Thomas Aquinas (1225–1274) for Aristotle, and St. Augustine (354–430) for Plato. St. Augustine, who was contemporary with the collapse of the Roman empire, was the greatest of the Church Fathers and the greatest influence on Christian thought in the pre-medieval period. St. Thomas was the greatest of the Scholastics of the Middle Ages, most responsible for the shift of Christianity from Platonism toward Aristotelianism, and almost

---

1. When I use the word "empirical" as attached to "science," I mean not simply based on experience but specifically based on controlled observation and measurement.

the "official" philosopher of Roman Catholicism from the four-
teenth to the middle of the twentieth century.[2]

The Augustinian-
Platonic Tradition

The Augustinian-Platonic tradition ascribed all "higher" psychological functions to the human *soul* as the divinely created
source of intellect, memory, and will, with only such "lower"
functions as sensations and the sense appetites being notably influenced by the body. Though the soul was the source of life and
sensation in the body (which by itself was inert and lifeless) as
well as of reason and will in man, it was viewed as entirely different in nature from the body or matter. For all who followed
Plato the true home of the soul was in a world apart from matter
in union with the divine, and the soul's existence in the body
was a kind of imprisonment or exile for it.

The Aristotelian-
Thomistic Tradition

The Aristotelian-Thomistic tradition, by contrast, saw the
union of soul and body as more natural and did not regard the
soul as debased by its being joined to the body. In fact, the soul's
primary function was to *animate* the body, not only making it
alive, but making it able to perceive sensory qualities, experience
appetite or desire, and move about freely, and giving to the
human being the rational powers of intellect and will.[3] To Aristotle and St. Thomas, soul (*psyche* in Greek, *anima* in Latin) was
not a supernatural but a natural entity, found wherever there
was life. Thus plants were said to have *vegetative souls* or animating principles which accounted for their being able to nourish
themselves, grow, and reproduce. Animals had *sensitive souls*

2. Etienne Gilson, *The Spirit of Medieval Philosophy,* trans. A. H. C. Downes
(New York: Scribners, 1936).
3. Thomas Aquinas, *In Aristotelis Librum De Anima Commentarium* (1266–68;
Turin: Marietti, 1948).

which enabled them not only to live organically but also to have sense perception and appetites, while man's *rational soul,* in addition to mediating the vegetative and animal functions, enabled human beings to think conceptually or abstractly and to exercise free will. This was a systematic, experientially based, and logically articulated view that was a far cry from primitive animism.

Galileo and Newton and the Mechanical Conception of Nature

The whole notion of soul or psyche as an animating principle, not only in man but especially throughout the rest of nature, ran into strong opposition in the seventeenth century with the growth of the mechanical conception of nature. This was the notion that the only realities needed to explain all the events of nature were matter and motion; that there was no need to postulate faculties or formalities or powers or agencies to explain natural phenomena, that this kind of assumption actually got in the way of understanding nature. No doubt the most important figure in the development of this concept was Galileo (1564–1642), for Galileo not only showed that the detailed examination of mechanical phenomena such as falling bodies, swinging pendulums, and planetary motion would reveal important facts about nature that ancient and medieval thinkers like Aristotle and the Scholastics had misunderstood, but also insisted that the application to the study of mechanical processes of the quantitative-mathematical method would facilitate the development of a true science of nature that would also yield to mankind an undreamt-of degree of control over natural phenomena. In his *Dialogues Concerning Two New Sciences* (1638) Galileo advised: *Measure everything. What you cannot measure directly, measure indirectly.*[4] Beyond that he urged that measurements be analyzed mathematically and their regularities summarized in algebraic equations that had the force not just of factual statements but of scientific laws. Galileo was

---

4. Galileo Galilei, *Dialogues Concerning Two New Sciences* (1632; trans. H. Crew and A. De Salvio, New York: Macmillan, 1914).

thus the founder of the modern science of mechanics and the one who set the stage for Newton's towering synthesis of physics and astronomy in the latter part of the seventeenth century, a system that would endure virtually without modification for more than 200 years. Newton's *Principia* (1687)[5] brought to fruition Galileo's vision of the universe as a master mechanism ruled by mathematical laws; Newton even invented a new branch of mathematics, the differential calculus, to set forth the laws of motion governing all the bodies in the universe from the falling apple in his orchard to the turnings of the most distant stars. One qualification must, nevertheless, be noted. Newton was not a pure mechanist, positing the existence of only matter and motion. In a fashion not too different from the ancients and the Scholastics he did postulate the existence of native powers of attraction and repulsion in things (notably the force of gravity), and in addition to solid matter he assumed the existence of an elastic medium called the *ether* through which the attractive and repulsive forces and various other energies between bodies could operate. But all force for Newton was expresed by movement or the tendency to movement, so that we can still say that in Newton the mechanical conception of the universe, at least in a broad sense, came into full and impressive bloom.

Descartes and Dualism

The man who was to exert the greatest influence on the seventeenth century's conception of psychological functioning, however, was not Newton but René Descartes (1596–1650), a younger contemporary of Galileo, a mathematician, experimentalist, and, above all, philosopher who accepted entirely Galileo's mechanical conception of the world.[6] Given matter as extended mass, to which God had originally imparted motion, said Descartes, all the phenomena of nature could be explained by me-

5. Isaac Newton, *Philosophiae Naturalis Principia* (1687; Cambridge, Mass.: Harvard University Press, 1972).

6. René Descartes, *Discourse on Method*, in *Great Books of the Western World*, ed. R. M. Hutchins, vol. 31 (1637; Chicago: Benton, 1952).

chanical laws. At the same time, however, as a religious man
Descartes was concerned to safeguard the conception of the soul
as a non-material entity responsible for man's intelligence and
freedom. Descartes attempted to preserve both Galileo's mechanism and the Christian notion of the non-materiality of the soul
by depriving the human soul of any animating function, separating it thereby from the body, and making it a pure *mind* whose
essence is *to think*. Here we have a reaffirmation of Platonism
regarding the radical alienation of the soul and body, but couched
in purely intellectual terms. Body, which according to Descartes
is at the basis of everything in the world except human thinking, is pure extension or space-occupying mass, inert except
for the motion which God imparts to it. Mind is utterly alien to
body; its principal ideas are derived from God rather than from
the world of matter, and mind is so identified with the non-
material act of pure thinking that it is only because of faith in
God's trustworthiness that our thinking self is even sure that a
material world exists. As far as psychological functioning is concerned, then, Descartes regards human thinking as altogether
different from any material phenomenon, though man's sensory
and locomotor powers are purely mechanical in operation, and
the cognitive and motivational functions of subhuman animals,
their apparent perception and memory and desire and emotion,
are really only the automatisms of robots. An ape therefore, to
Descartes, is far more like a clock than it is like a man, however
human-like it might seem to be. On the one hand, then, Descartes exalts the activity of mind far above any material function,
while on the other hand he sees psychological activities such as
sensory perception and appetition as entirely mechanical in nature. Was Descartes exaggerating the independence of the soul to
stay out of trouble with the Office of the Inquisition which, in
Descartes's own lifetime, had forced Galileo, under threat of tor-
ture, to recant his views on the movement of the earth around
the sun? There is no evidence to call into question Descartes's
sincerity or integrity, though he was unquestionably concerned
with the reaction of Church authorities to his unorthodox views
and withheld publication of several of his works on that account.

Certainly, Descartes's dualism did much to mitigate his mechanism.

Hobbes and Materialistic Mechanism

Interestingly, however, the man who pushed the mechanical conception of nature to its farthest extreme in the seventeenth century was not a scientist at all, despite his admiration for Galileo, and (despite his self-image) even less of a mathematician, but an English political philosopher, Thomas Hobbes (1588–1679). Hobbes argued that human thinking and motivation could be described as mechanical activities in common with everything else. Perception is thus nothing but motion in the head, transmitted by the motion of objects impinging on our sense organs. When the motion is fresh and lively we have sensation or perception; when the motion is relatively weaker and less lively we have imagination or conception; and when that motion is transmitted to the heart, it interacts with the vital motion there and becomes pleasure or pain, and gives rise accordingly to desire or aversion.[7] Reasoning for Hobbes is simply the association of images, based on our having experienced certain things together (association by *contiguity*), so that it too can be understood as nothing more than a compound or complex motion.

Locke

The exquisite simplicity of Hobbes's materialism was not, it would seem, quite persuasive to a still basically Christian public, so the philosopher who was most influential in shaping the final form of the seventeenth century's conception of psychological functioning was not Hobbes, but the more moderate and temperate "man of common sense," John Locke (1632–1704). Though neither a mathematician nor empirical scientist himself, Locke had for Newton a regard bordering on reverence and believed that an approach like Newton's could be applied anal-

7. Thomas Hobbes, *Leviathan* (1651), in *The English Works of Thomas Hobbes,* ed. W. Molesworth, vol. 4 (London: Bohn, 1839–45).

ogously to the understanding of human mental life. Locke was suspicious of a priori systems of philosophy such as those of Descartes and the continental philosophers influenced by him like Spinoza and Leibniz. In particular, Locke rejected Descartes's notion that certain ideas were innate or at least not derived from experience, arguing that the first principle of all understanding was the recognition that our knowledge without exception comes from experience, that our mind at birth is a blank tablet or *tabula rasa*.[8] Locke thus restored the Scholastic principle that there is nothing in the intellect that was not first in some way in the senses.[9] A whole host of succeeding thinkers in the British Isles (Berkeley, Hume, Hartley, and James Mill are the best known) followed Locke in this matter, thereby earning for the group the title "British empiricists." We should note, nonetheless, that not one of these men was an empiricist in the scientific sense, and their psychology was essentially a philosophical rather than an empirical one.

Locke himself, like Galileo, Descartes, and Newton, regarded some kinds of experience as more "objective" and trustworthy than others. He thus accorded principal value to the quantitative or measurable aspects of the world as we experience it, contending that characteristics like size and shape and motion and number are truly objective in the sense that they are found as such *in* things. These characteristics he called *primary qualities*. On the other hand, color and sound and taste and odor (*secondary qualities*) are not found as such in things, but are rather the effects *in*

8. John Locke, *An Essay Concerning Human Understanding* (1690; Oxford: Clarendon Press, 1924).

9. Aristotle agreed that the mind was a blank tablet at birth, though the axiom "Nothing is in the intellect, etc." derives from medieval Aristotelianism rather than from Aristotle himself. At all odds, this doctrine, which the Platonists in every age have tended to oppose, is often designated "psychological empiricism," an unfortunate term since it is easily confounded with "empirical psychology," to which it bears only the faintest relation. I shall refer to the doctrine that all knowledge is derived from experience as *epistemological empiricism*, a position held by many thinkers who had no connection with empirical science and certainly not with empirical psychology. Regarding the latter terms, recall that "empirical" does not mean simply "based on experience" but on that particular kind of experience involving controlled observation and measurement.

us of the primary qualities. This doctrine of the primacy of the quantitative was Locke's concession to the mechanical conception of nature. But Locke was neither a materialist nor a mechanist as far as psychological functioning is concerned. As I have indicated, he believed that one could apply a kind of Newtonian reasoning to the analysis of the "human understanding," as he preferred to call the mind. One accomplished this by first identifying the unit of mental function (the *idea*), corresponding analogously to the ultimate particle in the material world, and, second, by investigating the forces or powers that enable the human understanding to combine in various ways the ideas it derives from experience.

In the introduction to his *Essay Concerning Human Understanding* Locke made clear that by *idea* he meant "whatsoever is the object of the understanding when a man thinks." Despite its surface plausibility, this definition has so many hidden implications that it needs to be examined very carefully. In the first place, the definition shows that Locke has not departed as far from Descartes as his criticisms of innate ideas might lead one to expect, since it separates thinking or mental process almost totally from engagement with physical reality. By making the idea the *object* of thought rather than the *act* of thought, *that which* we know rather than *that through which* we know something outside the mind, it shuts the mind up in itself in Cartesian fashion, allowing it no direct commerce with the world. More curious than the definition itself were the ease and rapidity with which it was accepted as axiomatic by so many of Locke's contemporaries and successors. "To begin with, what we know is our ideas" sounds very reasonable, and Locke himself is such a paragon of sober judgment that no one would suspect him of either laying or falling prey to a subjectivist trap. Yet the many who followed Locke in this matter would have great difficulty in bridging the chasm which he had created between our ideas and reality, even though there is no doubt that Locke was a *realist* in intention, believing that certain ideas (those corresponding to "primary" qualities) are faithful reproductions of characteristics found in the objects of the material world. Indeed, Locke's belief in the validity of our ideas was in certain regards so great that he was convinced that one could understand a great deal about the world around us simply by studying our ideas of things.[10]

Whatever reasons prompted Locke to define the idea as the object of knowledge, the definition introduced a critical weakness into his realism for the anti-realists to exploit. Twenty years after the appearance of Locke's *Essay,* Berkeley would argue on Lockean premises that since what we know is an idea and ideas exist only in a mind, we have no reason for thinking that certain ideas are more objective than others. Inasmuch as we cannot imagine a thing having size and shape without color, for example, we cannot say that size and shape are found in things and color only in our minds. In truth, said Berkeley, all three exist only in minds and there is no justification for supposing that material substance exists as anything but a collection or association of ideas in our mind.[11] As remarked above, by focusing on ideas as the object of knowledge, Locke and those who, like Berkeley, followed him in this definition saddled succeeding generations of thinkers with the problem of how one gets from the knowledge of one's ideas to the knowledge of reality, a pseudoproblem, the multiplicity of whose pseudosolutions has bedeviled psychology and epistemology ever since.

The Association of Ideas

Another consequence of the British empiricists' preoccupation with ideas—particularly with the pictorial representations of things in our fantasy—was to give to the combining and separating or *association of ideas* an absolutely primary role in the analysis of

10. This conviction is a cardinal tenet of *psychologism*—another term that has no necessary reference to psychology. It is an attitude widely shared among the British empiricists. Thus Berkeley held, as noted below, that because we could not imagine a shape without any color, shape could not exist without color; and Hume argues that since we have no idea of an inner self or mind, there is no reason to suppose that a thinking self or mind exists. Psychologism and "indirect perceptionism," the doctrine that we perceive our ideas directly and things only indirectly, thus tend to be linked historically and, to some degree, logically.

11. George Berkeley, *A Treatise Concerning the Principles of Human Knowledge* (1710), in *The Works of George Berkeley,* ed. A. C. Fraser (Oxford: Clarendon Press, 1901).

human psychological functioning. In the nineteenth century, among the last of the British empiricists, the German sensory physiologists, and many of the first experimental psychologists, thinking *is* the association of ideas and the association of ideas is thinking. Now the association of ideas was by no means a new doctrine even in the seventeenth century. Aristotle had dealt with it in the fourth century B.C., but, unlike our nineteenth-century psychological forbears, he had regarded it as an interesting but entirely subsidiary aspect of mental life. The most important kind of thinking to Aristotle was directive thinking, concerned with solving theoretical and practical problems. Given certain premises or antecedent conditions, he asked, how do we draw the correct or valid conclusions to which they lead? Aristotle devoted two books to the laws governing this kind of relationship and thereby established the disciplines of formal and material logic. In his *Ethics* and in his *Politics* he also dealt with the problems of practical decision-making, of identifying the correct means to achieve a desired end. Deriving the correct conclusion from the premises given or the appropriate means for the end sought was the kind of association in which Aristotle was most interested, though he did recognize that one notion may call up another even though the two are not connected either logically or instrumentally. He refers to this secondary kind of association in his little book *On Memory and Reminiscence.*[12] To the notions of similarity and contrast, which Plato had mentioned as favoring recall of one thing given another, Aristotle here added the important factor of *contiguity,* and indicated that this was operative both in spontaneous remembrance and in deliberate attempts to recall partially remembered material. (If I want to recall X more clearly, I envision surrounding circumstances—V, W and Y, Z.) Even Aristotle's notion of contiguity is thus affected by his concern with directive thinking, in this case, deliberate recall. Contrast this with the modern notion of contiguity as set forth by Hobbes in his *Human Nature* (1650):

> The cause of the coherence or consequence of one conception to another is their first coherence or consequence at that time when they

12. Aristotle, *De Memoria et Reminiscentia,* trans. G. R. T. Ross (New York: Arno Press, 1973).

are produced by sense: as for example, from St. Andrew the mind runneth to St. Peter, because their names are read together; from St. Peter to a stone, for the same cause; from stone to foundation, because we see them together; and for the same cause, from foundation to church, and from church to people, and from people to tumult: and according to this example, the mind may run almost from anything to anything.[13]

Notice that what Hobbes is cataloguing is not directive but aimless thinking, of a kind that today might be termed "free associating" or "daydreaming." It is curious that the British and other associationists paid little attention to the adaptive activity of thinking, to the logical and practical use of thought in problem-solving, but were taken up with the passive process of association. Indeed, as associationistic thought progressed, it became less and less attentive to any active element in the thinking process. Thus the last of the classic associationists, James Mill, who published his *Analysis of the Phenomena of the Human Mind* in 1829, would argue that neither "similarity" nor "contrast" nor "cause and effect" had any necessary part to play in the association of ideas and that the mere *co-experiencing* of certain elements (contiguity) provided the basis for all our thinking.[14] To Mill the mind was simply a passive mirror, reflecting our experiences in the same order in which they had originally occurred.

Leibniz and Thinking as Activity

During all this period (from the late seventeenth century well into the nineteenth century) there was developing and circulating what might be called a minority view of thinking. Interestingly, this view was confined almost entirely to the German-speaking world, though its founder, the philosopher-mathematician Gottfried Wilhelm Leibniz (1646–1716), like most educated Germans of his day, wrote in French. Leibniz went even further than Descartes in insisting that mental activity was a unique phenomenon

13. Thomas Hobbes, *Human Nature, or the Fundamental Elements of Policy* (London: Bowman, 1650).

14. James Mill, *Analysis of the Phenomena of the Human Mind* (1829; London: Longmans, 1869).

that could in no way be reduced to mechanical processes; and he could not agree with Descartes that subhuman animals were robots without perception or feeling or that the material world in itself was inert and lifeless. Leibniz is very clear, in any case, that human perception is different from anything else in nature because it involves *consciousness*. Our cognitive activity is far more than the simple registration of sensible qualities: it is *apperception* because we not only perceive characteristics but are conscious or reflectively aware of our perception and of ourselves as perceiving. Even if we were able to identify precisely the brain activity concomitant with this apperception, that would in no way describe or identify the conscious state itself. The latter is a qualitative, not a measurable or quantitative, phenomenon that can only be described by the person who experiences it.

In his *New Essays Concerning Human Understanding* Leibniz wrote against Locke's psychological (or more properly, epistemological) empiricism, contending that the maxim "Nothing is in the intellect which was not first in the senses" had to be modified by the addition of four critical words: "except the intellect itself" (three words in Latin, *nisi intellectus ipse*).[15] He thereby stressed the pre-presence of the intellectual power itself as necessary to the understanding of anything presented by experience. It is thus that Leibniz is at the head of an originally minor but eventually important tradition which emphasizes the activity of the mind as contributing to knowledge, as opposed to the intellectual passivity favored by the classical associationists. This *intellectual activist* tradition extends from Leibniz through Christian Wolff to Kant, from Kant to Hegel and Herbart; and from the middle of the nineteenth century on, it is influential above all with Brentano and the two traditions that issued from Brentano, the psychological tradition that includes Stumpf, Külpe, and the Gestalt school, and the philosophical tradition represented above all by Husserl and Heidegger.

There are in Leibniz's position, it must be confessed, many weaknesses. He is a Platonist, almost an animist, and a believer in

15. Gottfried Wilhelm Leibniz, *Nouveaux essais sur l'entendement Humain* (1765), trans. A. Gideon, *New Essays Concerning Human Understanding* (Chicago: Open Court, 1916).

innate ideas, and his penchant for naive theological speculation made him an object of ridicule during the eighteenth-century "Enlightenment" and leaves his thought unpalatable to many moderns. Yet Leibniz was a great mathematician, independently discovering the differential calculus (for which Newton received virtually all the credit), and an innovator in psychology. His analysis of perception as involving degrees of increasing awareness, including his recognition of the existence of unconscious perceptual states (which he called *petites perceptions*), not only has a very modern ring but also decisively influenced the pioneering experimental psychology of Fechner in the 1850s and 1860s. No other thinker of his era had Leibniz's appreciation of the spontaneity and dynamic nature of intellectual function, and no analysis of conscious perception as irreducibly different from the mechanical matched his for phenomenological clarity and depth.

Leibniz's ideas were indirectly far more influential than is ordinarily recognized. His notions of intellectual power and spontaneity and the primacy of consciousness, for example, entered importantly into the pedagogically systematic thinking of his disciple, Christian Wolff (1679–1754), whose writings became the basis for the standard textbooks of philosophy over the next 200 years.[16] Kant, for example, had been thoroughly grounded in Wolff's curious synthesis of Leibnizian and Scholastic principles. More Leibnizian than Scholastic was Wolff's *rationalism* (as opposed to empiricism), according to which the mind had the power of grasping the essence of things independently of sense experience. Kant appears to have gone along blithely in this rationalistic belief until, as he confessed, David Hume woke him from his "dogmatic slumber." Even the Jesuits of the eighteenth and nineteenth centuries were crucially affected by Wolffian notions, accepting his scheme for the classification of the branches of philosophy (e.g., general and special metaphysics, rational and empirical psychology), a scheme that had no precedent in the Aristotelian-Thomistic tradi-

16. Christian von Wolff, *Lateinische Schriften*, 11 vols. (1732 ff.; New York: Hildesheim, 1979). This work includes volumes on ontology, cosmology, empirical psychology, rational psychology, theology, practical philosophy, and moral philosophy.

tion but that was still being used in American Jesuit colleges as late
as the 1940s! Though the influence of Wolff was neither mainstream nor entirely benign, it was nonetheless profound and pervasive.

Kant's Answer to Hume

As chief heir to the problems of both the Cartesian rationalists
and the British empiricists, and as the philosopher whom many
today consider the greatest since Aristotle, Immanuel Kant (1724–
1804) was certainly in the mainstream of European thought.
Kant's primary interest was not in human psychological functioning as such, but after reading Hume he was convinced that an epistemological analysis of human knowing was absolutely indispensable for the understanding of truth, reality, causality, and all that
is embraced by the science of nature. It is with the problem of
knowing viewed in this way that his major work *The Critique of Pure
Reason* is concerned.

Hume (1711–76) had carried Locke's empiricism to the extreme
and had pushed mental life even farther from direct contact with
substantial reality than had Berkeley. If all our knowledge comes
from experience, he reasoned, then there are no necessary or un-
changeable truths. What we know is only what happens, and there
is no compelling reason why anything happens just the way it does.
Much of what we think of as necessary knowledge (like the law of
cause and effect) is only a consequence of habitual expectation.
Repeatedly we experience *A* followed by *B,* so when we see *A,* we
expect *B*. But that is only the subjective habit of the mind: we do
not see *A* cause *B,* nor the influence of *A* on *B,* nor even *A* and *B* as
things in themselves. Our mental states are of two kinds, forceful
and lively ones called *impressions* (which include both sensations
and emotions), and faint images of these impressions which Hume
calls *ideas*. And these impressions and ideas are all we know. Beyond these, to be sure, one might point to the repeated *association* of
certain ideas with each other. In his first major work, *A Treatise of
Human Nature* (1739),[17] Hume regarded this association of ideas as

17. David Hume, *A Treatise of Human Nature* (1739; Oxford: Clarendon Press,
1896).

a "gentle force" analogous to the Newtonian law of attraction, but reference to this combinatory power is conspicuously absent from his later writings. From his last great work, *An Enquiry Concerning the Human Understanding* (1748),[18] it is clear that for Hume there are no forces or powers but only experienced events. What is most remarkable about these events is that certain of them are experienced with other events called *feelings* (such as hope and fear, desire and aversion, joy and grief), and Hume devotes considerable effort and ingenuity to an introspective analysis of the emotions. However, as far as any of our mental states putting us in touch with any underlying reality of a material or mental nature was concerned, Hume remained a complete sceptic.

That scepticism seemed to Kant to strike at the very foundations not only of our Christian moral heritage but of Newtonian science as well. Both "the starry heavens above" and "the moral law within," the two experiences which Kant regarded as the most compelling and meaningful in life, would alike be nullified if David Hume were right. But how could Hume be confuted without bringing back the rationalism of Leibniz and Wolff? This, Kant saw, was the problem, and for it he conceived a brilliant and profound solution. Not a psychological solution, to be sure, since the problem was, as I have indicated, an epistemological problem, but a solution that was to have important implications for psychology and for every other intellectual discipline. The solution goes as follows. Empiricism is right; all our knowledge begins with experience and without experience we know nothing. But the rationalists are partially right too; by its predetermined nature our faculty of knowledge gives to the raw materials of experience the sensible and intelligible quality of human perception and understanding. The "faculty of knowledge" is, then, no mere passive mirror reflecting things just as they impinge on it. It shapes and structures the raw material of sensory data into spatial and temporal experience. Space and time are perceptual forms intrinsic to the cognitive apparatus which enable us to experience things as in some place and at some time. Newton had made space and time absolute and infinite. Kant makes them absolute (if not infinite) by regarding

18. David Hume, *An Enquiry Concerning the Human Understanding* (1748; Oxford: Clarendon Press, 1902).

them as a priori forms of sense which cause us to experience reality always as spatial and temporal.

In comparable fashion, such attributes as reality, unity, causality, and necessity, which Hume had banished from the world of experience, are restored by Kant as necessary intellectual forms or categories which render the spatiotemporal data of perception intelligible. Like space and time, causality, unity, etc. are not in things, but in our way of conceiving them: they are laws of the mind. What we know results from the conjunction of an unknown thing-in-itself (*Ding-an-sich*) with the sensible forms (space and time) and the categories of the understanding (unity, reality, causality, necessity—some twelve in all).[19]

Thus did Kant "save" reason and intelligibility from the abyss of empiricist scepticism. It was a salvation, however, that seemed to many hardly better than the damnation threatened by Hume. To Kant the rational and the intelligible were "built into" the nature of the mind, but thereby were even further removed from reality (in the sense in which that term is usually understood) than in Hume's scheme. For it is Kant's contention that reality in the objective sense is not only in fact unknown, but in principle unknowable. It is hard to imagine a more radical empiricism.

As far as psychology is concerned, nonetheless, there is no doubt that Kant struck a mighty blow for the spontaneity and creativity of intellectual activity. Our thinking is by no means the simple function of experience, since *what* we think depends crucially on the intrinsic structure of our mental apparatus. This was a sophisticated and plausible kind of *nativism* which would deepen and extend Leibniz's insights and pose a serious challenge to associationism. Even contemporary psycholinguistics has been influenced by Kant's thinking in this matter.

Kant was no prophet regarding the future of empirical psychology as a science. Indeed he saw no future for it, since in his view it was impossible either to measure or to experiment with mental processes. How, he asked, could there be a science without measurement or experimentation? Fechner and Wundt would do a

19. Immanuel Kant, *Kritik der reinen Vernunft* (1781), trans. N. K. Smith, *Critique of Pure Reason* (London: Macmillan, 1929).

great deal to counter this pessimism, but to this day there are those who contend that psychology is not and never will be a science in the sense in which chemistry and even biology are sciences. This is a question to which we shall return.

Kant also sought epistemological justification for man's commitment to the *moral law* by positing that a sense of morality is universal, guaranteed by our intuitive grasp of what he called the "categorical imperative," which is stated as follows: *Act so that the principle of your action could by your will become a universal law of nature.*[20] Here again, however, it is the nature of human moral judgment, rather than the nature of things, that commands this maxim, a subjective necessity at best. Kant's final word is thus principally on the side of empiricism. What we know is the *phenomenon,* the appearance; what we need and desire and hope for, even demand, is the *noumenon,* the underlying reality which only intellect could understand and which would sustain our moral sense. This, alas! is forever outside the compass of pure reason and belongs to that complicated order of wishful thinking that Kant in his moral intensity ennobled with the title of "practical reason" (*praktische Vernunft*). Even the most admiring of his successors regretfully but firmly refused to take the latter notion very seriously.

Herbart and the Dynamic Unconscious

The man who in 1809 succeeded to Kant's chair at the University of Königsberg, Johann Friedrich Herbart (1776–1841), disagreed with Kant on many issues but was an equally strong proponent of the dynamic nature of the intellect. Unlike Kant, Herbart was primarily interested in psychological functioning per se. He believed firmly that psychology was a science and could be most profitably applied to the improvement of education. In fact, Herbart is better known for his contributions to education than to philosophy or psychology. Nevertheless, his contribution to the development of scientific psychology was great. He combined many

20. Immanuel Kant, *Kritik der praktischen Vernunft* (1788), trans. L. W. Beck, *Critique of Practical Reason* (Chicago: University of Chicago Press, 1949).

influences from the past and had a distinctive effect of his own on a number of later thinkers of consequence. Like Leibniz, Herbart stressed the unity and the spontaneity of the soul or mind, but like Locke he believed that a kind of Newtonian mental dynamics best described the actual interplay of ideas. Borrowing from Newton, too, and in pointed disagreement with Kant, he attempted to prove that mathematics could be applied to the understanding of mental activity. Ideas, he argued, are of varying intensity and may oppose each other in a manner analogous to the forces of nature, a situation that lends itself nicely to mathematical analysis of the Newtonian type,[21] which Herbart proceeded to apply freely, if rather inconclusively, to the interaction of ideas. Herbart's beliefs that psychology could not be an experimental science and that the study of the physiology of the nervous system could cast no light on the nature of the mind were not destined to be influential. Fortunately, there were other Herbartian ideas that were more happily fated.

Herbart believed that the force or intensity of ideas can be judged by their *clarity,* and when an idea is opposed by stronger (i.e., clearer) ideas, the weaker or increasingly less clear idea slips below the threshold (*limen*) of consciousness. The idea does not cease to exist, however, but continues to push toward consciousness, and if some of the ideas opposing it are themselves excluded from consciousness by other ideas, the previously inhibited or repressed idea will rise above the threshold and thereby return to consciousness. Thus introduced into the description of the mental life is the extremely important conception of a *dynamic unconscious.* Herbart construed this notion in purely cognitive terms, to be sure, so one should not over-stress the resemblance to the Freudian dynamic unconscious, which is principally a motivational conception. Nevertheless, the principle was established and its novel applications made possible by Herbart's pioneering analysis. The notion of *limen of consciousness,* likewise, which would play a key role in Fechner's foundational work in psychophysics, derives from

21. Johann Friedrich Herbart, *Lehrbuch zur Psychologie* (1816), trans. M. K. Smith, *A Textbook of Psychology* (New York: Appleton, 1891).

Herbart. With it also goes the notion of the *continuum of conscious-unconscious* (understood as *clear-unclear*): looking backward, a revival of Leibniz's *petites perceptions,* and looking forward, a precursor of Fechner's negative or subthreshold sensations and of his application of Weber's law to above-threshold values of sensible intensities. If Fechner's psychophysics is the beginning of experimental psychology, it is difficult to see how it could have come about without the influence of Herbart, a man who regarded experimental psychology as an impossibility.

Finally, we should note that Herbart saw more in the mental life than individual ideas; there was also the dominant pattern of conscious ideas (or apperceptions) which Herbart called the "apperceptive mass." It was the ruling assemblage of ideas that determined the admissibility of new ideas to consciousness, so that Herbart regarded the notion of the apperceptive mass as momentously significant for learning and education. For all his dynamism and practicality, Herbart continues one aspect of the associationist tradition, that of focusing on ideas in themselves and in their mechanical interplay rather than on their relation to the external world and to the conduct of human life. The Cartesian split between mind and matter thus endures in Herbart, as in Locke and Hume and Kant, and *psychologism* (in the sense of studying reality by examining our ideas of it) and indirect perceptionism are in him very much alive.

One effort to heal (or annul) this split is the double aspect theory of mind and body whose leading proponent in the seventeenth century was Benedict Spinoza (1632-77). In Spinoza's world view there is only one substance, and both thought (mind) and extension (matter) are aspects of it.[22] Mind and body are thus the same substance viewed in different ways; each is real but neither is independently real. This is in sharp contrast with the Cartesian dichotomy between mind and matter which, as we have seen, had driven many to deny one or the other. Thus Berkeley denied the reality of

---

22. Benedict Spinoza, *Ethica: More Geometrico Demonstrata* (1677), trans. W. H. White and A. H. Stirling, *Ethics Demonstrated in Geometrical Order* (London: Oxford University Press, 1927).

material substance, while Hume had refused to accept as real what the Cartesians called the "self" or "mind."

Fechner

No nineteenth-century thinker was more poignantly aware of the need to bring the material and the mental together than Gustav Theodor Fechner (1801–87). Fechner was both a physicist and a spiritualist, a distinguished exponent of the mathematical approach to electrical currents and other physical phenomena and a firm believer in the importance of the spiritual factor, not only in man but throughout the whole realm of nature. The materialists had contended that living substances were only machines, that life and sensation and emotion and thought were simply material processes. There is truth in this contention, said Fechner; not the dismal denial of the spiritual mouthed by the materialists, however, but the implicit affirmation that sense and life and thought are found in everything, in plants and animals and even in the distant stars![23] This seemed to his contemporaries to go farther than Spinoza's double aspect theory and to represent a return to a primitive animism or the hylozoism of the early Greek philosophers, like Thales and Anaximenes. He did insist upon the reality of both the spiritual and the material aspects of the world, though he also recognized that it was quite possible for people to look at only one aspect and ignore the other. One could, in short, take the "night view" (*Nachtansicht*) and fail to appreciate the deeper validity of the "daylight view" (*Tagesansicht*), which recognizes the spiritual within the material. What Fechner hoped to do was to prove the materialists scientifically wrong by demonstrating experimentally the commensurability (or co-measurability) of the physical and the psychic. The intuitive insight that revealed the general way in which this could be accomplished came to him while he was in a dreamlike state in October 1850. The solution was to demonstrate that there was a precise proportion between the increase in physical energy of a sensory stimulus and the intensity of the resulting

23. Gustav Theodor Fechner, *Zend-Avesta oder Gedanken über die Dinge des Himmels und des Jenseits* (1851; Leipzig: Fischer, 1922).

sensation. If a geometric increase in the magnitude of the stimulus produced an arithmetic increase in the intensity of the sensory experience, the postulated proportion would be demonstrated, and Fechner proceeded to offer what he regarded as precise quantitative data that allowed no other interpretation. The threshold of consciousness (*Reizlimen*) could be calculated, he said, by determining the point at which initial awareness of the stimulus is reported: this was the base or zero point of sensation. Next, the unit of increase could be determined by having the subject report at what higher degree of intensity the increase itself became noticeable. This was the famous "just noticeable difference" (j.n.d.) or differential threshold (*Differenzlimen*), the unit of measurement for increases in the intensity of the sensation which Fechner, following Weber, believed were always proportional to the magnitude of the original stimulus—in general a matter of common sense and common observation, but given new authority by the claim that this relationship could be supported by precise measurement. "If you need two more candles to make a ten-candle light look brighter, you'll need twenty to do the same thing for a hundred-candle light" becomes "The differential intensity threshold is proportional to the measured value of the original intensity" or, better still, "$\Delta I/I = k$."[24]

Note carefully, however, that what is being measured is but a tiny aspect of the mental life, namely, 1) the minimum intensity required for consciousness of the stimulus to take place, and 2) the unit of increase in intensity of the same stimulus which is barely detectable. Notice, too, that there is no question of using psychophysical methods to compare different sensory qualities or modalities, and certainly no question of measuring anything beyond the simplest stimulus intensities such as brightness for color and loudness for sound. It follows that Fechner's claim that the *Elemente der Psychophysik* set forth "an exact science of the functional relations or relations of dependency between body and mind" must be regarded as pure hyperbole. After more than a hundred years of psychophysical experimentation, we know that Fechner's revision of

24. Gustav Theodor Fechner, *Elemente der Psychophysik* (1860), trans. H. E. Adler, *Elements of Psychophysics* (New York: Holt, Rinehart, and Winston, 1966).

"Weber's law" is not a scientifically valid generalization for sensory intensities as a whole but the rough description of a tendency that holds only for the middle range of audible and visible stimuli. The Weber-Fechner fraction can tell us nothing about the quality of sensation (such as color or pitch) and very little about any other sensory modality (such as taste or smell or tactile sense). Fechner proved that quantitative methods have a valid application to the analysis of certain kinds of sensation. As a consequence, the refined detailing of psychophysical measurement remains a respected undertaking in precise experimental methodology, unfairly pilloried by the ultra-humanistically oriented as "eye, ear, nose, and throat psychology." Perhaps William James was too harsh in concluding that "the proper psychological outcome" of all Fechner's "thoroughness and subtlety" was *just nothing,* but many of us would have to agree that the light cast by psychophysics on the nature of cognitive functioning is itself barely above threshold intensity.

Wundt

No one in the nineteenth century had a more profound and carefully articulated conception of the distinctive nature of psychological functioning than Wilhelm Wundt (1832–1920), who is generally credited with being the father of experimental psychology as an academic discipline. To Wundt the psychic event is a unique kind of experience (*Erfahrung*), and whether we endeavor to correlate that event with measured physical stimuli (as did Fechner), with neural and other psychological conditions (as did the sensory physiologists, such as Helmholtz), or with distinctively human customs, institutions, and forms of conduct (which Wundt himself dealt with in his popular psychology or *Völkerpsychologie*),[25] the event itself in its mental or psychic quality is incontestably certified by immediate experience. In several important respects Wundt was the major beneficiary of the British empiricist heritage, accepting Locke's notion of the *idea* as the experienced unit of mental

25. Wilhelm Wundt, *Völkerpsychologie* (1911), trans. E. L. Schaub, *Elements of Folk Psychology* (London: Allen and Unwin, 1916).

function and including under the term "idea," again like Locke, sensory perceptions as well as fantasy and memory images. In the broad sense, too, Wundt is an associationist, acknowledging that the growth of mental life is in great part dependent on the compounding of ideas. Unlike Locke, however, Wundt rejected the idea as the ultimate unit of analysis not only because it was based on the more elementary process of sensation, but because sensation could be analyzed further into its distinct if inseparable components, quality and intensity. Moreover and most important, Wundt rejected the associationistic notion of ideas as the passive reflections of sense experience, insisting that in the combining of psychic elements there operated a "principle of creative synthesis," so that the characteristics of the compound are by no means the mere sum of the characteristics of the elements. This notion resembles the "mental chemistry" of John Stuart Mill rather than the "passive contiguity" of his father, James Mill, and also seems to anticipate Lloyd Morgan's notion of "emergence" and Bergson's "creative evolution." No doubt Wundt owes much to Leibniz and Herbart in this matter—like them, he places great stress on the act of apperception as an integrative and clarifying force in human mental life. To Wundt, apperception is a spontaneous process which involves the act of *attention* and which elevates perception to clear and distinct comprehension. It is also apperception that brings sense experience to the level of *feeling,* feeling itself being described as the "mark of the reaction of apperception upon sensory content."[26] Like sensation, too, feeling is regarded as an elementary kind of experience. Wundt devoted much effort to the analysis of feeling, an effort remarkable for its combination of almost pure phenomenology and experimental assiduity. The result was the famous three-dimensional theory of feeling which Wundt believed to be supported by the most careful introspective particularization and by a great deal of apposite experimental evidence. Ingenious and intriguing and in certain areas quite persuasive, the tridimensional theory of feeling has curiously found few supporters even among Wundt's staunchest disciples such as Titch-

26. Wilhelm Wundt, *Grundriss der Psychologie* (1896), trans. C. H. Judd, *Outlines of Psychology* (New York: Stechert, 1902).

ener. Phenomenologically, Wundt made out a good case for two of his three dimensions: 1) pleasant–unpleasant and 2) excited–calm; but he was never able to prove the distinctness of 3) tense–relaxed from the second dimension (the supposedly supportive experimental witness proved uncertain at best).

Wundt was well schooled in philosophy, especially logic, and his multivolume *Textbook of Logic* went through four editions, extending over forty years.[27] His position on the nature of psychological function was therefore a self-consciously philosophical one, and it would be doing him no injustice to designate him a psychophysical parallelist of the strict observance. Mental events and neurophysiological events were to him in one-to-one correspondence, but there was no interaction between them and no possibility of substituting one for the other. The perfect concordance between the bodily and the mental made it legitimate to study their intercorrelations and even to postulate the existence of a psychic concomitant for every neural process and a neural concomitant for every psychic process. Thus, since the nervous system is made up of neural units, there must be similar units of psychic "structure." If these are not evident to immediate experience, we may be sure that they can be reached eventually by using appropriate methods of analysis. The quantitative aspects of our sensory experience can be approached by Fechner's psychophysical methods, though the qualitative aspects of experience can be dealt with only by a direct analysis of our own self-observations (*Selbstbeobachtungen*) or introspections. There is no doubt in Wundt's mind that the facts of consciousness always have complex nerve processes as their physiological substrate, but *in our experience what we know directly and immediately is the sensory or feeling quality, not its physiological foundation.* It is to the analysis of this qualitative aspect of sensory and feeling experience that Wundt devotes his most intensive efforts. However phenomenological these efforts may initially seem to be, it is clear that Wundt's analysis is guided by certain metaphysical and epistemological presuppositions that are decidedly non-phenomenological in nature. The first of these is that there *are* units of men-

---

27. Wilhelm Wundt, *Logik: Eine Untersuchung der Prinzipien der Erkenntnis und der Methoden wissenschaftlicher Forschung,* 2 vols. (Stuttgart: Enke, 1893–95).

tal function, corresponding to units of neural structure and process, which are the same for all and to which all "higher" mental processes can be reduced. Wundt also assumes that the method of self-observation (*Selbstbeobachtung*) or introspection can reveal not only the units of mental function but the manner in which they are combined or connected and the laws governing their compounding. Most striking of all is Wundt's belief that individuals can be trained to describe exactly the content of experience, that they can do this without reference to the significance of the experience or to external objects, and that with sufficient training virtually perfect agreement between self-observers can be obtained. Psychology, Wundt argues, unlike physics, deals with *immediate* experience and makes no inferences or mediate judgments about external reality[28] or even about any mind or mental agency "behind" the ideas. Mind is process, not substance, and there is no mental entity or mind stuff over and above the "actuality" (i.e., *activity*) of ideas. Even self-observation (*Selbstbeobachtung*) does not imply the reality of any mental self, distinct from the sum of mental states: "having an idea" and "being conscious of an idea" are to Wundt one and the same thing. Wundt also rejected the notion of psychic or mental energy and saw the activity of mind as lawful but not causal in the physical sense,[29] thus putting distance between his ideas and those of Fechner and all the psychophysiological theorists (including such strange bedfellows as Helmholtz and Freud) who regarded energy as a concept equally applicable in the physical and mental orders.

Brentano

A different conception of the nature of psychological functioning and of the nature of psychology as a science was very consciously advanced by Franz Brentano (1838–1917) in his book *Psychology*

28. Notice that Wundt too embraces indirect perceptionism. What we know immediately is our own mental states (sensations, ideas, feelings, etc.), and our knowledge of physical processes is mediate or inferential. External reality remains external.

29. Edwin G. Boring, *A History of Experimental Psychology*, 2nd ed. (New York: Appleton-Century-Crofts, 1950), pp. 335–37.

from an Empirical Standpoint (*Psychologie vom empirischen Standpunkte*).[30] This work was published just a year after the appearance of the first part of Wundt's *Principles of Physiological Psychology,* and was quite consciously offered as an alternative to it. Brentano, a former Dominican priest, had been thoroughly trained in Aristotelian philosophy as well as in the Scholastic philosophy stemming from St. Thomas Aquinas (also a Dominican priest), and he saw in Aristotle's notion of the active intellect (*nous poietikos* or *intellectus agens*) as developed by the Scholastic philosophers in the Thomistic tradition a valuable insight into the nature of intellectual activity that the associationists and even Wundt had failed to appreciate.

Wundt was primarily concerned with the *content* of our ideas, and though he accorded special status to the intellectual activity of apperception (following Kant and Herbart), his principal interest was in the quality contained in the idea (i.e., its qualitative content). Thus when Wundt examined the perception of red, it was to the "idea of red" that he turned, a content different from the "idea of green" or the "idea of middle C." Brentano, on the other hand, wanted to stress above all the *activity* of sensory perception, not the image or idea of red or middle C, but the act of seeing red or hearing middle C. The representation (*Vorstellung*) of red or middle C is certainly not nothing, but it is not a color or a sound but a mental act, and the "red" or "middle C" as grasped has an existence *within* (*Inexistenz*) the mental act; not physical existence, but what the medieval Scholastics called "intentional being" (*ens intentionale*), the mode of existence proper to the mental representation of an object.[31] To characterize this existence Brentano favors the expression "immanent objectivity," which conveys the point

---

30. Franz Brentano, *Psychologie vom empirischen Standpunkte* (1874), trans. A. Rancurello, D. B. Terrell, and L. McAlister (New York: Humanities Press, 1973). The term "empirical" (*empirisch*) as employed by Brentano means simply "based on experience" and does not imply either controlled observation or the direct manipulation of independent variables (the hallmark of the experimental method). It would, therefore, be more precise and less confusing to translate his word *empirisch* by the English "experiential," though up to now no one has undertaken to do so.

31. The term "intentional" here has nothing to do with "intention" in the sense of purpose or aim. On this account I have translated it below as "referential."

that the mental act always has an object but *remains within* (from the literal meaning of "immanent") the subject. For Brentano it is thus the mental phenomena that are the true object of psychology. What saves this position from subjectivity is the contention that mental phenomena always refer to objects. What Brentano calls the object's *intentionale Inexistenz* may then be translated as "referential existence within" (the mental phenomenon), which means simply that a mental act always refers to an object. The object may be concrete like a colored surface, abstract like beauty or justice, or even entirely imaginary like a golden fleece, but object there must be, distinct from the mental act that refers to it.

There are three kinds of mental acts or mental phenomena recognized by Brentano, and each of these contains an object within itself referentially. They are 1) *vorstellen* (representing, imagining, ideating); 2) *urteilen* (judging, evaluating, recognizing); and 3) *lieben und hassen* (literally, "loving and hating," but including all manner of emotions, feelings, wishing, desiring, intending, even choosing). For each, the same principle holds: in the idea (*Vorstellung*) something is represented; in judgment (*Urteil*) something is affirmed or denied; in hate (*Hass*) something is hated, in desire something desired, etc.

British empiricism and associationism had, as noted above, burdened the mental life with a double weakness: 1) being limited to the passive reflection of sensory experience, yet 2) remaining cut off from extramental reality. Virtually all European thinkers after Locke had accepted one or the other of these burdens as a kind of intrinsic debility or original sin of human nature. Brentano, however, rejected outright the first limitation and argued, regarding the second, that though mental phenomena are essentially different in nature from anything physical, this does not prevent us from grasping in outer perception (*äussere Wahrnehmung*) the data of the external sensory world.

Brentano strove most vigorously to remove the stigma of passivity from the human psyche. Not only is the mind active, as Kant and Herbart and Wundt had recognized; *its acts are its being.* Berkeley, concentrating on the idea as the *object* of knowledge, had concluded that the being of sensible objects is in their *being perceived* (*esse est percipi*). To Brentano, on the contrary, the idea (*Vorstellung*)

is the act of apprehending, not the state of being apprehended (not
esse est percipi, but *percipere est agere*—to perceive is to act). In a certain sense, as Brett says, the color and the seeing are one. An act of
apprehending, however, is meaningless unless there is something
apprehended. The action is mental but the object—even an imaginary object—is distinct from the mental act of apprehending it.

When it comes to deciding whether the object of thinking, as it is
being thought about, has an existence apart from thinking, Brentano adopts a complex position and might seem to be making a significant concession to idealism. Mental phenomena, he says, are
perceived only in inner consciousness. It follows that the object of
this inner consciousness is itself something mental, the object as it
"exists within" the mind (*In-existenz*). It would seem, however,
that Brentano saves his position from subjectivity by recognizing
the legitimacy and priority of external perception whose object is,
in his words, physical (*physischen*). In his way, therefore, Brentano
does break the "double bind" which psychologism and associationism had drawn around the human mind. Insisting that thinking exhibits its own distinctive and dynamic mode of existence
("intentional" or "referential") and admitting that our inner
awareness is not directed to an extramental object, he nevertheless
avoids the pitfalls of indirect perceptionism, the notion that what
we apprehend directly is only in our minds. From his Aristotelian
background Brentano had learned that our perceptions are not primarily that which we know but that in which or through which we
know other things. Yet Brentano also stressed the power of the
mind by which it knows immediately and surely its own inner
states, insisting on the indispensability and even infallibility of the
inner perception of our own ideas, judgments, feelings, and volitions.

This inner perception, he argued, must be carefully distinguished from inner observation (*Beobachtung*) of which Wundt
made so much. Brentano agreed that ideas (*Vorstellungen*) were always conscious, but he rejected outright Wundt's contention that
having an idea and being conscious of an idea are one and the
same. On the contrary, we do not and cannot apprehend clearly an
idea in the act of having it. Wundt's *Selbstbeobachtung* would require
us to be discriminatively aware, for example, of an emotion in the
midst of that very emotion, a simple impossibility. We cannot

stand outside our ideas, feelings, and other mental acts and observe them as we would physical events. At most, we can train ourselves to recall clearly our experiences immediately after we have had them. Reconstruction must take the place of self-observation, introspection become retrospection.

Brentano's Heirs and Assigns

Among psychologists, the first and most important of Brentano's immediate heirs was Carl Stumpf (1848–1936). Stumpf had been something of a child prodigy in music, and his precocity in other areas was also remarkable. He was a Ph.D. at twenty and a full professor at twenty-five, and all at the same University of Würzburg where at the age of seventeen he had become a disciple of Brentano.

Stumpf turned to good effect his musical talent and training in the development of his classic work in music, the two-volume *Tonpsychologie*,[32] which featured both experimental method and a complex and sophisticated phenomenology. The latter marked a notable departure from the strict elementarism and psychophysical methodology which Wundt championed, and brought down Wundt's wrath on Stumpf's head in a series of scathingly critical articles.[33] Though upset by the acrimony of Wundt's criticism, Stumpf stuck to his guns, arguing strongly that phenomenology is antecedent to psychology and a propaedeutic or pre-science (*Vorwissenschaft*). Tones as experienced, not as reconstructed by Wundtian "structural" introspection or psychophysical analysis, are instances of phenomenological data and they must be accepted as such. For example, because *consonance* (a fusion or merging of tones) produces a new and unified experience, it must be regarded as a fundamental musical phenomenon in its own right. Indeed, as Stumpf saw it, consonance is the most fundamental of experiences for the esthetic appreciation of music—a value which did not harmonize with the rigidities of Wundtian laboratory method. In

---

32. Carl Stumpf, *Tonpsychologie*, 2 vols. (Leipzig: Hinzel, 1883 and 1890).
33. Wilhelm Wundt, "Ueber Vergleichungen der Tondistanz," *Philosophische Studien* 6 (1891): 605–40; ibid., vol. 7 (1892): 298–327, 633–36.

addition, according to Stumpf, we must recognize the reality of psychic functions like perceiving, willing, and desiring (corresponding to Brentano's *acts*) as proper subject-matter for psychology.[34] Stumpf also postulated other types of psychological functioning which went beyond the usual limits of empirical psychology but still had an empirical—or at least an experiential—base, such as *relations* between phenomena and between functions, notions later to be explored by the Würzburg school.

Stumpf added to Brentano's cognitive acts of perceiving (*vorstellen*) and judging (*urteilen*) the act of conceiving (*begreifen*). Like Brentano, Stumpf saw emotions and motives as bipolar (joy and sorrow, seeking and avoidance, accepting and rejecting), though unlike Brentano, he argues for the existence of a special category of "feeling-sensations" (*Gefühlsempfindungen*) as the phenomenological basis for emotions, highly plausible and well-documented positions that seem not to have been as influential as their merit would justify.[35]

Stumpf held professorships at Würzburg, Prague, Halle, Munich, and Berlin and had among his students or assistants Köhler, Koffka, and Husserl. Admired by all, Stumpf had few or no disciples, perhaps in part because his greatest gifts were in music and phenomenological analysis, areas of competence that were easier to acclaim than to imitate. Like his friend and confidant, William James, he stimulated his students to think for themselves and to apply to other fields ideas which he may have suggested to them, and most important, he served as a link between Brentano and experimental psychology.

Külpe and the Würzburg School

Beginning as a Wundtian of strongly positivistic persuasion, Oswald Külpe served as Wundt's assistant and as an instructor

---

34. Carl Stumpf, "Erscheinungen und psychische Funktionen," in *Abhandlungen der preussischen Akademie der Wissenschaft* (Berlin: 1906), no. 4.

35. Carl Stumpf, "Ueber Gefühlsempfindungen," *Zeitschrift für Psychologie* 44 (1907): 1–49.

(*Privatdozent*) in Wundt's laboratory courses for six years (1888–94). Despite his admiration for Wundt, Külpe was not entirely convinced that Wundt was right in restricting the experimental method to cognitive processes having sensory content, excluding thereby the experimental investigation of the "higher" thought processes. In 1885 Ebbinghaus had demonstrated that memory could be studied experimentally, and Külpe did not see why the method of experimental self-observation could not be extended to such mental phenomena as conceptualization, decision-making, problem-solving, even reasoning. When Külpe published his first major work (*Grundriss der Psychologie*)[36] in 1893 he had not developed sufficient material on the thought processes to say anything about them, but in 1894 he was made professor at Würzburg and thereby given the opportunity to develop his own philosophy of research investigation, instruction, and criticism.

Most of the books written by Külpe during his fifteen years at Würzburg (1894–1909) were philosophical in character, but he did stimulate and encourage his experimental staff to study at length such matters as judgment (Marbe), conceptual thinking (Watt), emotionally toned attitudes (Orth), purposive thinking and its relation to action (Ach), and acts of thinking as they are given in the actual everyday experience of thoughtful men (Bühler). Based on these investigations and on his own participation in many of them as a subject, Külpe believed that the primary emphasis should be placed on *acts of thinking* (*Denken*) rather than on content of *thoughts* (*Gedanken*). These acts of thinking were impalpable or "imageless" (*unanschaulich*), a position reflecting Brentano's view and diametrically opposed to that of Wundt. We may recall that Wundt, while acknowledging the importance of mental activity and deploring the passive associationism of James Mill and the British empiricists, had insisted that experimental investigations must focus primarily not on acts or functions but on sensory content.

The investigations inspired by Külpe and carried out in his laboratory were strikingly integrated by their concern with the higher

---

36. Oswald Külpe, *Grundriss der Psychologie* (1893), trans. E. B. Titchener, *Outlines of Psychology* (London: Sonnenschein, 1901).

mental functions. The importance of Külpe's influence, despite the meagerness of his own publications of an experimental nature, may be inferred from the fact that after his departure from Würzburg in 1909, the school ceased to be an identifiable force in psychology. Under Külpe's guidance, at any rate, his staff found a good deal of evidence indicating the significance of thinking as an impalpable or "imageless" process. I will briefly summarize some of the more striking of these investigations.

In studying word associations, Mayer and Orth found that certain stimulus words gave rise to "states of consciousness" or "conscious attitudes" (neither phrase quite captures the sense of the German *Bewusstseinslagen*) which could not be described as perceptions or images or even volitions, but which had a definite influence on the subject's response.[37]

In the same year (1901) as that of Mayer and Orth's study, Marbe set out to investigate a related but distinct problem: the psychological nature of the *judgment*.[38] Judgment had been traditionally regarded by logicians as the fundamental act of thought because it is the simplest unit which can be designated as true or false. Logically, the judgment is easy to define as the act of affirming or denying a predicate of a subject, but how is this basic intellectual process to be categorized psychologically? Individuals obviously recognize that they are making judgments and the observer can detect both verbal and nonverbal expressions of judgments, such as the verbal answer "three" or the raising of three fingers in response to the question, "How much is seven minus four?" But Marbe was unable to discover any psychological criterion of judgment, there being no content in consciousness to tell us why the judgments that we make are judgments, even though we are clearly conscious of making them. The fact of our being conscious of this must itself be described as a not-otherwise-characterizable "state or attitude of consciousness" or *Bewusstseinslage*.

Some three years later, Watt attempted in the Würzburg lab-

37. Adolf Mayer and Johannes Orth, "Zur qualitätiven Untersuchung der Assoziationen," *Zeitschrift für Psychologie* 26 (1901): 1–13.

38. Karl Marbe, *Experimentelle-psychologische Untersuchungen über das Urteil, eine Einleitung in die Logik* (Leipzig: Engelmann, 1901).

oratory to study thinking by having his subjects accomplish *tasks* (*Aufgaben*) calling for conceptualization.[39] For example, subjects were asked to identify an object by giving the class to which it belonged, to cite an example of another object in the same class, of an object in a different class, and the like. Immediately after each response to a task or *Aufgabe,* subjects were instructed to introspect at length and each subject was asked to concentrate on one of the following: 1) the period before the appearance of the stimulus word; 2) the period of the appearance of that word; 3) the period of the search for the reaction word; and 4) the period of the appearance of the reaction word. It had been expected that the third period would provide most of the conscious content of the introspections, but such was not the case. For the most part, conceptualization would go on "automatically," if only the task or *Aufgabe* had been adequately understood and accepted by the subject in the preparatory period, i.e., *before* the appearance of the stimulus word. It is the *Aufgabe,* and not some image or picture, that gives direction or *set* (*Einstellung*) to the subject's responses.

Another member of the Würzburg "family," Narziss Ach, undertook to extend the investigations of Watt to the realm of practical decision-making and action.[40] How, he asked, does the *Aufgabe* carry over into action? His investigations led him to conclude that there is present to consciousness in the first place a goal-idea (*Zielvorstellung*). From this goal-idea proceed influences which determine the character of the subject's subsequent response. If the task is to subtract the smaller from the larger of two numbers to be shown or to lift the right index finger from a telegraph key when the letter *E* appears, the task (*Aufgabe*) as understood becomes a goal-idea (*Zielvorstellung*) which gives rise in turn to a specific "determining tendency" (*bestimmende Tendenz*) toward a certain action. Determining tendencies, according to Ach, are unconscious; in this respect they are apparently not different from Watt's "sets" (*Einstellungen*), which also appear to work unconsciously. Like the

39. Henry J. Watt, "Experimentelle Beiträge zur einer Theorie des Denkens," *Archiv für gesamte Psychologie* 4 (1905): 289–436.

40. Narziss Ach, *Ueber die Willenstätigkeit und das Denken* (Göttingen: Vandenhoeck and Ruprecht, 1905).

set, too, the determining tendency appears to be a directive factor in thinking and in overt action.

Though the determining tendency is not conscious, Ach argues that it has an effect upon consciousness, so that there is a consciousness or awareness of the act as being determined. This awareness (*Bewusstheit*) also, however, is lacking in sensory content and is therefore impalpable or imageless (*unanschaulich*).

Ach illustrated the effects of the determining tendency by experiments in posthypnotic suggestion. Under hypnosis, for example, a subject was told that he would later be shown two cards, each with two figures on it. "When you see the first card," he was instructed, "you will name the sum; when you see the second card, you will name the difference of the figures." After a short lapse of time the subject was shown a card with the figures *6* and *2*. He immediately said "eight." Shown a second card with the figures *4* and *2*, he immediately said "two." The subject admitted to a "felt need" to say "eight" on presentation of the first card. This is an essentially impalpable or imageless awareness of the *effect* of the determining tendency. The determining tendency is itself thus not experienced but inferred in order to account for the directiveness or purposiveness of our thinking. The determining tendency is effective, Ach contended, without conscious memory of the task and it is what knits the mental process into a functional and structural whole. Thinking of this sort is deliberately willed and as such quite distinct from fantasy or reverie. It is the determining tendencies, Ach believed, that rule out irrelevancies and prevent fortuitous considerations from distracting the course of our thinking, a position that calls to mind Aristotle's emphasis on the directive nature of our thinking and that would later be reflected in the clinical description of normal and abnormal thinking found in the work of Eugen Bleuler and Paul Schilder.[41]

41. Schilder, writing in the 1920s, and free from the associationistic restrictions that limited Bleuler's earlier and otherwise brilliant analysis of schizophrenia, saw the absence of the *determinative idea* (which keeps fringe elements from obtruding into the normal thought process) as characteristic of schizophrenic thinking. The "determinative idea" sounds like a condensation of the "goal idea" (*Zielvorstellung*) and the "determining tendency" (*bestimmende Tendenz*) of Ach. See P. Schilder, "On the development of thoughts," *Zeitschrift für gesamte Neurologie und Psychiatrie* 59 (1920): 250.

Against the associationistic notion of thinking as passive combinations of sensory images ruled by mere contiguity, the Würzburg school thus offered a view of human thinking as a dynamically unitive and purposive, but impalpable, process, having both conscious and unconscious aspects. No one of the Würzburg partisans was more firmly committed to a phenomenological refutation of associationism than Karl Bühler. We will conclude our summary of the Würzburg school with a brief review of his position.

In a series of papers published in 1907 and 1908 Bühler undertook to describe our actual experience when we deal intellectually, not with trivialized, routine, or rote memory problems, but with a series of tasks each of which calls for careful and original thinking.[42] Bühler chose for subjects individuals of unquestionable intellectual superiority and employed with them a method of extensive questioning (known as the *Ausfrage* or "interrogation" method). He reported at length the results with two men of distinction in psychology, Külpe himself and the psychologist-critic Ernst Dürr, later editor and reviser of Ebbinghaus's major textbooks in psychology. The kind of problems that Bühler posed to these thinkers called for logical, theoretical, and historical interpretation, for example, Was Eucken right when he argued that we could not know the limits of our knowledge unless we somehow transcended those limits? Can we comprehend with our thought the nature of thought? What is the law of association in its simplest form? Is it possible that the atomic theory can ever be proved untrue?

When the two subjects endeavored to describe how they arrived at answers to these questions, they were struck by the presence of peculiar states of consciousness similar to what Marbe had designated by the term *Bewussteseinslagen,* and which Külpe and Dürr described by such words as "doubt," "astonishment," "recollection," and "expectation." Bühler concluded that these were instances of consciousness of the process of thought itself in experience. Most of this kind of experience has no sensory quality or sensory intensity, and though impalpable, is by no means inaccessible

42. Karl Bühler, "Tatsachen und Probleme zu einer Psychologie der Denkvorgänge. I. Ueber Gedanken; II. Ueber Gedankenzusammenhänge," *Archiv für gesamte Psychologie* 9 (1907): 297-305.

to awareness, consisting for the most part of the very turning points of the thought process in actual experience. It has identifiable attributes which can be present in greater or lesser degree, e.g., certainty, vividness, clarity. These experiences are states of "knowing," of "consciousness that," clear, assured, and stable, nothing so fragmentary, sporadic, and at the mercy of chance as are images. Külpe's and Dürr's introspections (or better, perhaps, "retrospections") showed that these men made complex judgments without any accompanying images, for instance, the realization that the thought of the future is not the same as the future itself, and the intellectual remembrance (prompted by a statement of the presumed conflict between purpose and chance) that Darwin had considered chance the explanation of purpose.

Another type of thought-experience emerging frequently in Bühler's experiments is "consciousness of a rule" (*Regelbewusstsein*). Thus Dürr was able to affirm the possible refutability of the atomic theory because he knew in general how questions regarding the truth or falsity of scientific theories are solved. The coming to mind of grammatical rules when we are hesitant about how to say something correctly is another example of *Regelbewusstsein*.

A synoptic awareness of some segment of intellectual history, like "the pre-Socratic philosophy which Plato opposed," can be clearly present without any image or without even any consciousness of a rule. And sometimes the very dispensability of images may itself become the object of an imageless insight, such as that reported by Külpe: "It struck me that one could think of the objects of the external world such as material bodies . . . in immediate fashion without having to form images of them." Külpe seems therewith to have realized that the overemphasis of the image in German and British thought was a consequence of *indirect realism* or, as it was called in the late nineteenth century, *presentationism,* the doctrine that one does not experience the world directly but the presentations (*Vorstellungen*) engendered by it or their reproductions. Brentano had attacked indirect perceptionism, and Külpe affirmed that Brentano's criticism was supported by experimental self-observation. Therefore there is no reason in experience to accept Locke's definition of the idea as "whatsoever is the *object* of the understanding when a man thinks." The idea is the instrument of understanding, not its object.

Agreeing in part at least with Ach's notion of the determining tendency, Bühler contended that the known relation between one thought and another, or between thoughts and the task (*Aufgabe*) as understood, guarantees the unity and directiveness of the thought process, setting off deliberate thinking from fantasy or reverie.

Bühler also contrasts word-for-word memorization with intellectual memory of the kind needed to retain the general sense of a passage of literature or to recognize a proverb as equivalent to, though not identical with, a previously heard one, for example, "One looks to the cask when the wine escapes into the cellar" as similar to "When the calf is stolen, the farmer repairs the stall."

All in all, despite some methodological carelessness, the Würzburg school's case for the existence and importance of thinking as a conscious state, distinct from any combining or permuting of images with sensory content, is a strong one that has been independently supported by the work of Binet in France and Woodworth in the United States, as well as by that of many thinkers directly influenced by the Würzburg school, including Thomas Verner Moore, A. A. Grünbaum, and Horace B. English.[43]

Gestalt Psychology

Against the elementarism and reductionism of the classical associationists, the movement known as Gestalt psychology argued for the primacy of organized wholes (*Gestalten*) as these are given in ordinary experience. The philosopher Christian von Ehrenfels had stressed the importance of the "Gestalt quality" (*Gestaltqualität*) more than twenty years before the perceptual experiments of Max Wertheimer (1912) that formed the basis of the Gestalt movement

43. Alfred Binet, *L'étude expérimentale de l'intelligence* (Paris: Schleicher frères, 1903); Alfred Binet, "Le bilan de la psychologie en 1908," *Annee Psychologique* 15 (1909): viii–ix; "Le bilan de la psychologie en 1909," *Annee Psychologique* 16 (1910): iv–v; Robert S. Woodworth, *Experimental Psychology* (New York: Henry Holt, 1938), pp. 786 ff.; Thomas Verner Moore, "The Process of Abstraction," *University of California Publications in Psychology* 1 (1910): 73–197; Abraham Grünbaum, "Ueber die Abstraktion der Gleichheit: Beitrag zur Psychologie der Relation," *Archiv für gesamte Psychologie* 12 (1908): 340–480; Horace B. English, "An Experimental Study of Certain Initial Phases of the Process of Abstraction," *American Journal of Psychology* 33 (1922): 305–50.

in psychology.[44] It was against Wundtian elementarism indeed that von Ehrenfels, who had been a student of Brentano at Vienna, argued to the effect that the specific nature of an experience is not determined by the elements of that experience but rather by the structure or pattern (*Gestalt*) of their interrelationships. It is, as everyone knows, not the notes of a song that determine the melody, but their arrangement, so that the same notes rearranged make a different melody, while different notes arranged similarly yield the same melody, as when we play a song in a different key.

Two of the three founders of the Gestalt movement, Koffka and Köhler, had been exposed to the phenomenology of Stumpf, both taking their degrees under him in 1909, while Wertheimer had been earlier influenced by the perceptual phenomenology of Külpe, under whom he took his doctorate in 1904. Külpe had insisted, against Wundt, that many features of the world, e.g., space and time (or extent and duration), are directly perceived rather than "inferred" or "apperceived." A line is thus grasped perceptually as a whole and not as a series of segments; a duration is experienced as such and not as a succession of moments. Perception is thus not a compiling of discrete sensations but a unitary and instant process. In a flash of insight Wertheimer in 1912 realized that this same principle could well be applied to the perception of motion. It would follow then that movement would be immediately perceived visually rather than synthesized, as it were, from distinct visual sensations of a number of locations, along with kinesthetic sensations of accompanying eye movements. Wertheimer, using the stroboscope, showed experimentally that eye movements had nothing to do with the perception of motion, and that the latter was a distinct phenomenal experience, emerging immediately from certain sensory conditions even though it was by no means reducible to them.

Gestalt psychology thus began as a phenomenological theory of perception, but it was not long before leading Gestaltists extended their theory of organized patterns to include higher mental pro-

---

44. Christian von Ehrenfels, "Ueber Gestaltqualitäten," *Viertel Jahrschrift für wissenschaftliche Philosophie* 14 (1890): 249–92; Max Wertheimer, "Experimentelle Studien über das Sehen von Bewegungen," *Zeitschrift für Psychologie* 61 (1912): 161–265.

cesses (with particular emphasis on intellectual problem-solving). Nor was Gestalt theory content to remain a phenomenology of perceptual and other mental processes. Even in the original paper written by Wertheimer on the visual perception of motion, an effort was made to link Gestalt theory with the physical properties of the nervous system. All three of the Gestalt movement's leaders argued that the dynamic nature of perceptual and problem-solving processes was based on the dynamic properties of the brain, and that Gestalt psychology's greatest claim to scientific status was in its consonance with the contemporary physics of field theory, as opposed to Newtonian particle theory. There developed thus the famous theory of *psychoneural isomorphism* which holds that there is real, though not perfect, correspondence between the dynamic properties of the perceptual field and the excitatory characteristics of the brain field under conditions of sensory stimulation. Thus if we perceive light to move from one point to another in space, there must be a corresponding movement from one place to another in the brain. Despite many efforts to verify this principle experimentally (especially by Köhler), the bulk of neurophysiological evidence is *against* the notion of isomorphism between brain fields and perceptual fields,[45] while the Gestaltist's alleged correspondence between the insightful restructuring involved in intellectual problem-solving and the redistribution of energy in the brain (which tends to produce a condition of lowered tension) seems more like a metaphor than a testable psychophysiological theory.

The physicalism of the Gestalt thinkers aside, Köhler and Wertheimer do make some valuable observations on the phenomenology of the thought process in problem-solving.[46] Thinking only occurs, they argue, when a fresh *Gestalt* is formed. As envisioned, the problem-solving process effects an essential change in the originally disconnected experiences in order to form a new

45. Karl S. Lashley, Kao-Liang Chow, and Josephine Semmes, "An Examination of the Electrical Field Theory of Cerebral Integration," *Psychological Review* 58 (1951): 123–36; Roger Sperry, Nancy Miner, and R. E. Meyers, "Visual Pattern Perception Following Subpial Slicing and Tantalum Wire Implantation in the Visual Cortex," *Journal of Comparative and Physiological Psychology* 48 (1955): 50–58.

46. Wolfgang Köhler, *Gestalt Psychology*, 2nd ed. (New York: Mentor, 1947); Max Wertheimer, *Productive Thinking* (New York: Harper, 1945).

Gestalt, a "recentering" (*Umzentrierung*) leading to an "insight" (*Einsicht*) into the relations between the hitherto unrelated aspects of the "field." Thinking is therefore essentially creative. In support of this conceptualization, Wertheimer gives many strikingly plausible illustrations. Let us begin with one of his examples and go on to one or two additional illustrations.

Most people know that the area of a rectangle is the product of its adjacent sides. Thus: if in rectangle ABCD the adjacent sides are represented by AB and BC, the area of the rectangle is AB × BC. Suppose, however, that the angles of a somewhat similar four-sided figure are not right angles, though the opposite sides are still parallel and equal. We then have a parallelogram with adjacent sides AB′ and B′C′.

Let us suppose now that BC and B′C′ are the same length. How do we determine the area of the parallelogram? Considering the figures separately, we may see that AB and AB′ are not the same length, so that the relation of the area of the parallelogram to that of the rectangle is not clear. Suppose now we superimpose one figure on the other:

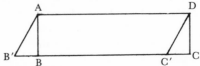

We know that the area of ABCD is AB × BC and we can now see that the triangles AB′B and DC′C are congruent and thus identical in area. The parallelogram AB′C′D can then be seen as adding one of these triangles to the rectangle ABCD and subtracting the other. The parallelogram is therefore identical in area with the rectangle and must equal AB × BC. In the parallelogram, the line

AB would represent not a side but an altitude (the perpendicular distance between the two horizontal sides). Its area therefore is either of its two horizontal sides multiplied by that perpendicular distance (AB × AD or AB × B′C′), which is the same as the area of the corresponding rectangle. The solution becomes evident when we combine the figures because we can then readily grasp the truth that the two triangles have the same area and the two four-sided figures likewise. This to the Gestaltists is the "recentering" (*Umzentrierung*) that results in the insight (*Einsicht*) that the two adjacent sides of the rectangle also provide the area of the corresponding parallelogram, which solves the problem.

A similar example may futher illustrate the phenomena of restructuring and insight. Take the ascending series of integers that are perfect squares: 1, 4, 9, 16, 25, 36, 49, . . . They are of course the squares of the integers 1, 2, 3, etc.

Integer	Square
1	1
2	4
3	9
4	16

Is there any rule governing the relation of the first to the second column other than the condition given that the numbers in the right-hand column are the squares of those in the left-hand column? Perhaps we might try restructuring by looking at the squares as sums rather than products. We can then see that $1 = 1 + 0$, $4 = 1 + 3$, $9 = 1 + 3 + 5$, $16 = 1 + 3 + 5 + 7$, $25 = 1 = 3 + 5 + 7 + 9$, etc. One remarkable fact that now stands out is that the integers whose sum makes up each of the perfect squares are all odd numbers. Once we have seen this, we can also see that the square of 2 is equal to the sum of the first two odd numbers, the square of 3 is equal to the sum of the first three odd numbers, the square of 4 is the sum of the first four odd numbers, and so on. If you have the patience to test it out, you will also find that the square of 100 (10,000) is the sum of the first 100 odd numbers, and the general rule is clear: N^2 = the sum of the first N odd numbers, where N is any positive integer.

Or consider the question: Why is it that every six-digit number made by repeating a three-digit number is evenly divisible by 13?[47] Thus $127,127 \div 13 = 9,779$; $484,484 \div 13 = 37,268$; $101,101 \div 13 = 7,777$. Try looking at such six-digit numbers from several perspectives: Is either of its three-digit components evenly divisible by 13? Not always. Is the sum of all the digits equal to 13? Again, not always. Is the sum of all the digits equal to a number divisible evenly by 13? This, too, is a blind alley, but it suggests another possibility. What is the relation of the first three digits to the second three? They are identical as digits but *not* as numbers, because the first three digits are in the hundreds of thousands place while the second three are only in the hundreds place. Thus 127,127 is one hundred and twenty seven thousand plus one hundred and twenty seven. The number 127,000 is $1,000 \times 127$, and 127,127 is $1,001 \times 127$. In like manner, 484,484 is $1,001 \times 484$, 101,101 is $1,001 \times 101$, and so on. The six-digit number whose second three digits repeat its first three is always divisible evenly by 1,001. And why is this number evenly divisible by 13? Because 1,001 is evenly divisible by 13, being equal to 13×77. The recentering of the problem around the relation between the three digits in the hundreds of thousands place and the three digits in the hundreds place leads inevitably to understanding why all such repetitive three-digit combinations are evenly divisible by 13, which is the problem to be solved.

In all these instances, the solution to the problem seems to depend on a restructuring of an original problem, the grasping of a new *Gestalt* which gives to the terms of the problem a new contextual meaning which in turn provides a ready means of solving the problem. The superimposing of the two geometrical figures enabled us to understand readily that the areas of the two figures had a common element and an additional identical element; the analysis of the odd integers making up the perfect squares, and, in our final problem, the analysis of the repeated integers "in place," made it easy to grasp a whole series of new relations. As Norman Maier (cited by Humphrey[48]) showed, instructing people in ways

47. George Humphrey, *Thinking: An Introduction to Its Experimental Psychology* (London: Methuen, 1951), pp. 168–70.
48. Ibid., pp. 178–79.

to promote the perception of new *Gestalten* or patterns can result in improvement in their problem-solving skills. To the understanding of that very important kind of thinking called problem-solving, it is clear that Gestalt psychology makes a genuine contribution. Despite its physicalistic preposessions, Gestalt theory does stress the creative side of human thinking. As Duncker notes, in creative problem-solving there is usually a series of progressive reorganizations in which aspects of the situation which before hardly existed at all psychologically, or existed only "unthematically" in the background, leap forward, gain prominence, acquire a figure or a theme, become a means to an end.[49]

Köhler liked to emphasize the notion that direction is given to problem-solving not by "determining tendencies" in the subject but by the self-adjustment of a system in stress, each phase of the process growing out of its predecessors, and only those mental acts occurring which will decrease the psychophysical tension of the system. Consciousness to him, as Lowry notes, is nothing but the "isomorphic phenomenal counterpart" of the underlying brain activity which, though not "mechanical," is entirely "automatic."[50] This, unfortunately, is to become so focused on the physicalistic model as to lose sight of many facts. In the first place, the crucial tension to solve the problem is not in the problem but in the person, for it is only the person who is capable of understanding, is motivated to act, becomes emotionally involved in finding a solution. Understanding, motivation, and emotion are psychic variables which are present in the situation only because they are present in the person who is in and concerned with the situation. Secondly, the element of *consciousness* (of purpose or goal, of meaning, of value) is not a resultant of the process but a major determinant of it, in the absence of which the descriptive understanding of the action of problem-solving would be impossible. In the third place, an entirely "automatic" process could in no way convey the distinction between creative or "productive" and purely reproductive thinking, a distinction so well described phenomenologically by Wertheimer. Though Gestalt theory was, as noted above,

49. Ibid., pp. 166 ff.
50. Richard Lowry, *The Evolution of Psychological Theory: 1650 to the Present* (Chicago: Aldine-Atherton, 1971).

rooted in phenomenology, it seems that it could hardly wait to embrace a physicalistic model by which it could transform psychological aspects of problem-solving, like restructuring and insight, into a kind of counterbalancing of physical stresses. That physical automatism is any closer to the reality of human thinking than elementaristic reductionism is far from clear, nor does it seem that physicalism has any more empirical support than other philosophical positions. Indeed, the extrapolation of physical methods from the physical to the behavioral sciences is on the whole a cardinal instance of the intrusion of philosophical biases into what should be matters of scientific data determination.

The part of Gestalt psychology most likely to endure, it would seem, is not its theory of neural isomorphism or its equilibrial extrapolations from physics, but its descriptive analysis of the thought process in creative problem-solving just as we experience it, a basically phenomenological exercise.

Husserl's Phenomenology

Unlike Stumpf, who befriended him and whom he greatly admired, Edmund Husserl (1859–1938) was a late bloomer. Starting out in mathematics and physics at the University of Leipzig, he was unimpressed by the lectures of Wundt in philosophy and psychology and transferred first to the Friedrich Wilhelm University in Berlin and then to the University of Vienna, finishing his doctorate in mathematics there in 1883. At Vienna, however, he came under Brentano's spell and determined to make philosophy his life work. In 1886 Husserl, on Brentano's recommendation, went to the University of Halle to become Stumpf's assistant and in 1887 became a member of the Halle faculty of philosophy as a *Privatdozent* (unpaid lecturer), a post he was to hold for fourteen years. He was thus forty-two years old before he received an appointment as associate (*extraordinarius*) professor at Göttingen, and it was during his years at Göttingen that he developed his systematic philosophical phenomenology. It was another fifteen years before he was offered a full professorship at the University of Freiburg. This was in 1916, by which time Husserl was fifty-seven years old. Hardly a meteoric rise! though by this time Husserl was so well known and respected internationally that it is difficult to believe that intellectually extraneous considerations played no role in the delayed recognition of his great contributions. Among possibly relevant factors are such personal characteristics as perfectionism, pride, and great insecurity, which contributed to his continual alternation from over-confidence in the value of his revolutionary insights to an almost masochistically self-disparaging humility. Nor can one ignore altogether the influence of anti-Semitism in the German university even in the early stages of his career, though the brutal humiliation to which he was subjected by the Nazis during his retirement years was another matter, made doubly bitter by the National Socialist sympathies of the man Husserl had nominated to succeed him at Freiburg, Martin Heidegger.

From Brentano, Husserl derived the notion of *intentionality* as the most distinctive feature of mental life, though he proceeded to develop this notion in ways with which Brentano could not agree. From Brentano, too, he accepted the ideal of philosophy as the most rigorous and critical and scientific of intellectual disciplines, an ideal that Husserl set forth with great passion and cogency in his 1910 article "Philosophy as a Rigorous Science" (Philosophie als strenge Wissenschaft) and which he continued to advance in his very latest writing.[51]

Husserl is above all a philosopher, a thinker of great depth and subtlety, at times undauntedly abstruse and complicated in his reasoning, but always dedicated to the purpose of doing complete justice to the data of experience, while acknowledging and safeguarding the creativity and uniqueness of mental life.

To Husserl the most important fact in the universe is the existence of *awareness* in the human being. For him this is the "wonder of all wonders," pure consciousness and the subjectivity that is its vehicle and that he liked to call the "pure ego." The *primal fact*

---

51. Edmund Husserl, "Philosophie als strenge Wissenschaft," *Logos* 1 (1910): 289–314; English translation by Q. Lauer, "Philosophy as a Rigorous Science," *Crosscurrents* 6 (1956): 227–46. Husserl's latest work, which was never finished, was *Die Krisis der europäischen Wissenschaften und die transzendentale Phänomenologie*, ed. H. L. van Breda (The Hague: Nijhoff, 1954) (condensed English translation by A. Gurwitsch in *Philosophy and Phenomenological Research*, vol. 16, 1956, pp. 380–99, and vol. 17, 1957, pp. 370–98).

(*Urtatsache*) is that *in man Being comes to self-awareness,* and it is the appreciation and elucidation of this fundamental truth that constitutes the heart and soul of Husserl's philosophical mission. Without human consciousness the universe remains forever mute and meaningless, but with consciousness the human subject in its very existence has the whole world present to it, and the whole world, in turn, is met by human consciousness. From the interweaving strands of this relationship Husserl was to fabricate the substance of his "transcendental phenomenology."

The designation "transcendental" is appropriate since many aspects of Husserl's system go far beyond the bounds of psychology as an intellectual discipline, even of philosophical psychology, and into the realms of logic, metaphysics, and epistemology. Husserl's own interest in psychology was great but rather specialized, being focused on phenomenological psychology as distinct from but related to both empirical psychology and philosophical phenomenology. The ultimate goal of Husserl's philosophical phenomenology was the achievement of "transcendental subjectivity" by which the absoluteness of conscious existence and the dependence of all transcendental reality on consciousness can be established. In Husserl's view such a philosophical phenomenology could supply the foundation of all knowledge. Phenomenological *psychology,* however, had a key role to play in the development of transcendental phenomenology, and that was to supply the first stage of phenomenological "reduction," the so-called "eidetic reduction" in which our analysis concentrates on the *psychological reality* of the conscious state, excluding or "bracketing" all reference to nonpsychological reality. This "eidetic" or phenomenological-psychological reduction, according to Husserl, also serves the purpose of clarifying the nature of psychological reality for the benefit of empirical psychology; for, without such clarification, empirical psychology tends inevitably to lose sight of its own proper object and to become mired in the extraneous parameters of the natural sciences. This in turn leads to the trivialization of the entire field of empirical psychology in the pursuit of "solutions" to pseudoproblems. Only reliance on phenomenological analyses will enable psychology to interpret correctly and evaluate critically the empirical facts discovered by its own investigations. The perfect antithesis of Husserl's position is that of the behaviorists, who insist that all reference to consciousness must be excluded before psychology can hope to achieve any scientific status, and Husserl lived long enough to appreciate the antithesis. To ignore the phenomena of conscious life *just as they are given in experience* is to abnegate the ultimate source of all knowledge in favor of physicalistic dogma. To Husserl, no matter how refined the measurement or how ingenious the experimental techniques employed by empirical psychology, all its efforts are meaningless without a clear grasp of *what it is that is being measured and correlated* in the first place. He argued that such a clear grasp can only come from a first-order phenomenological "reduction" or intellectual analysis which concentrates on psychological phenomena just as they are given in immediate experience without any attempt to relate them to nonpsychological reality, whether behavioral, physiological, or physical. As indicated above, phenomenological reduction parenthesizes or brackets even the existence of anything other than the conscious experience itself; this forms the basis of a purely descriptive psychology which does not go nearly as far as the transcendental phenomenological philosophy which is the capstone of Husserl's system, but provides a foundation and a direction to the empirical psychology pursued by Wundt and Stumpf and Külpe with whose work Husserl was well acquainted. Husserl saw this empirical psychology as capable of fulfilling a most important function but actually doing little to realize this capability. The deficiency was in no way due to its psychophysical and psychophysiological investigations themselves. Indeed, Husserl realized clearly that without such investigations psychology would not be dealing with psychological functioning as it actually exists, i.e., as imbedded in a physical world and characterizing a particular kind of physiological entity, the human being. When psychology takes its lead entirely from the natural sciences (by which he meant principally physical science and biology), it fails utterly to do justice to that which is most distinctive of the human being and *the most important phenomenon in the whole universe*. Here Husserl speaks from the perspective of transcendental phenomenology, according to which consciousness has its proper being in itself and constitutes a region of being essentially different from other beings. *All lived experiences* (*Erlebnisse*) are conscious, so that to overlook consciousness is to fail to understand that which is most characteristic of our human life,

namely, that it is a *conscious life*. The existence of consciousness is
thus far more directly and unassailably given than that of any
"external" reality; indeed, it is only through consciousness that
the existence of anything *else* is given to us. Consciousness is *intentional:* it is always consciousness of something, and Husserl here
goes farther than Brentano, insisting that intentionality is the very
essence of consciousness. Our consciousness is *openness to, relation to*
the whole objective world; at the same time consciousness is constantly *present to itself*. Even when we go through the process of
transcendental reduction, in which we suspend judgment regarding the
existence of everything in the world, including our own psychological ego—a deliberate act of what the ancient sceptics called *epoche*
(withholding)—our consciousness of the world (the world on
whose existence we are suspending judgment) remains, and with
that consciousness the pure ego which is conscious of itself as the
center of the stream of consciousness. When I see that my life *is*
consciousness of the world, I appreciate the absolute existence of
pure consciousness and I reach the reality of *transcendental subjectivity*. And Husserl does not hesitate to push his position to its ultimate metaphysical conclusion that: ". . . every imaginable being
. . . falls within the domain of trancendental subjectivity, as the
subjectivity that finally constitutes all sense and Being."[52] As
Levinas says:

> For Husserl it is the subjective world that is real; the physical world
> has reality of another degree . . . the origin of all being, including
> that of nature, is determined by the intrinsic meaning of conscious
> life and not the other way around . . . In summary, the existence of
> an unperceived material thing can only be its capability of being per-
> ceived . . . a possibility which belongs to the very essence of con-
> sciousness . . . A material thing . . . is relative to consciousness—to
> say that it exists is to say that it meets consciousness.[53]

Shades of Bishop Berkeley! Fortunately, we need not follow Husserl in these challenging idealistic speculations since they clearly go

52. Joseph J. Kockelmans, *A First Introduction to Husserl's Phenomenology* (Pitts-
burgh: Duquesne University Press, 1967), p. 224.
53. Emmanuel Levinas, *The Theory of Intuition in Husserl's Phenomenology* (Evanston: Northwestern University Press, 1973), p. 22.

far beyond the realm of the psychological into that of metaphysics and epistemology. It is only Husserl's insistence on the absolute distinctiveness and psychological primacy of the conscious life that is of moment for psychology. This is, as we have noted, his phenomenological psychology rather than his phenomenological philosophy.

In his lecture courses in 1925 and 1927 Husserl again stressed the need for a phenomenological psychology proper to supply the essential insights which could give meaning and direction to the research of empirical psychology. Such a phenomenological psychology, Husserl believed, could through reflective analysis (after the "eidetic reduction") provide us with a description of the essential nature and variety of lived experiences, reveal the psychological essence of the stream of consciousness, and give us some notion of the psychological ego as the center of our lived experiences.[54] Husserl realized how forbiddingly difficult such an analysis would be, however, and saw clearly how the physicalistic orientation of contemporary psychologists would discourage the attempt at any such analysis. In his last major writing, *The Crisis of European Science and Transcendental Phenomenology* (1936), Husserl argued that this "naturalization" of the psychical led to a confusion of experientially "lived" time with the spatialized time of physical science. It also led to a neglect of the "life-world" (*Lebenswelt*) which is the world as we immediately experience it in our everyday living. This *Lebenswelt* is not just the sensed world but the world open to the full range of human experience, intellectual, esthetic, emotional, sociocultural, and historical, and the world of practical meaning and value as well. The world of the physical sciences originates in the life-world, but in its efforts to "objectify" and "quantify" its data, science tends to forget its humble origins and its dependence on the uncritical interpretation of many aspects of everyday experience. Enthralled by the ideal of the physical sciences, psychology requires a phenomenological reduction in order to overcome the illusion of its own perfect objectivity and to recognize its dependence on the life-world. Subjecting the existence of

54. Herbert Spiegelberg, *The Phenomenological Movement* (The Hague: Nijhoff, 1969), vol. 1, p. 162.

this life-world and of all other types of external reality to a sus-
pension of belief (*epoche*), the first stage of the phenomenological
reduction, enables us to see our lived experience *qua* experience
and to inhibit our disposition to reify it in physicalistic terms. A
phenomenological reduction does not for a moment deny the existence of the physical; it simply "brackets" this assumption and
empowers our focusing on the psychological (or psychic) as such in
our experience. Nor does this reduction prevent a phenomenological psychology from accepting the quantification and empirical
analysis of the physical and the physiological correlatives of our
psychic states, such as the physical stimuli concomitant with our
sensory perceptions, or the physiological activities and conditions
concurrent with our motives and emotions.

Thus did Husserl set the stage for a new rapprochement between psychology and philosophy, a stage setting that was to evoke
little in the way of responsive role-playing from an empirical psychology, touchily prideful of its newly acknowledged scientific
status and beset by its own pre-adolescent conflicts. Husserl's insistence on the uniqueness and primacy of human awareness and
the necessity of a phenomenological approach to the understanding of human existence, however, was to call forth an initially enthusiastic response from the man whom many regard as the twentieth century's most philosophically learned and original thinker,
Martin Heidegger.

Husserl and Heidegger

Heidegger was never a pupil of Husserl's, though at one time he
had aspired to study under Husserl at Göttingen. For personal
(largely financial) reasons, Heidegger took his degree at Freiburg
in 1913 and was added to the faculty as *Privatdozent* in 1915, the
year before Husserl's accession to the Freiburg chair of philosophy. In Husserl's first year at Freiburg Heidegger was his assistant; then the younger man went off to complete his military ser-
vice. It was upon his return that the relation between him and
Husserl became very close, though it was more that of senior professor and junior colleague than of master and pupil. Husserl fully
appreciated Heidegger's brilliance and originality and looked to

the youthful scholar as his intellectual collaborator and spiritual heir. As early as 1919, however, and even when Heidegger was teaching a course in "pure" phenomenology, the distinctive components of his own orientation were becoming apparent. Heidegger had begun his master work, *Sein und Zeit,* by 1922, the year before he left Freiburg to accept a full professorship at Marburg.[55] Though Husserl disagreed profoundly with the deviations and limitation that Heidegger had introduced into his version of phenomenology, he continued to esteem the younger man's genius, and on the eve of his own retirement (in 1928) he nominated Heidegger to succeed him at Freiburg, believing him to be the only qualified person. By this time *Sein und Zeit* had seen the light of day and, despite its dedication to Husserl, the irreconcilabililty of the differences between these two great thinkers was absolutely evident.

The sticking point was the question of *transcendental subjectivity.* To Husserl this represented the final goal of all phenomenology, that which could transform philosophy into a rigorous science (*strenge Wissenschaft*) and which demonstrates that it is consciousness (*Bewusstsein*) that ultimately constitutes all meaning and all being. For Heidegger's basically anti-idealist bent, this was too much. He would grant that man's awareness of himself and other beings is the primary subjective fact, and in one sense definitive of that which is most distinctive of human existence, but he would insist that subjectivity as such is precisely *not* transcendent, that it tells us nothing about the *Being (Sein)* which is manifest both in the human being and the other beings of which he is aware. This Being (*Sein*) which is present in all entities or beings (*Seiendes*) has been the principal object of philosophical inquiry since time immemorial, and to Heidegger it is the question of this immanent but transcendent Being (*die Seinsfrage*) that remains the great challenge to philosophy. Heidegger's own central concern, moreover, is the problem of the *meaning of this Being.* To ignore this question seems to him an indefensible omission, to subordinate it to the problem of consciousness an inversion of the proper order. Being is more fundamental than consciousness. Indeed, consciousness is itself a

---

55. Heidegger had thus achieved before age thirty-five an academic status which Husserl did not reach until he was fifty-seven!

manifestation of Being since it is the act or state of *being* aware—an easier point to make in German, where consciousness is Bewusst-*sein*. To Husserl the "wonder of all wonders" was pure conscious-ness and the pure ego; but Heidegger asks: What is it that this sub-jective consciousness is aware of? To be conscious is to experience in human fashion, and the human being alone of all existing things experiences what to Heidegger is the "wonder of all wonders"— that there are things-in-being (*dass Seiendes ist*).[56] With Husserl, Heidegger holds that in man alone does Being come to self-aware-ness, and with Husserl too he acknowledges that human conscious-ness is openness to the whole objective world. What he cannot accept is the notion that our consciousness *constitutes* the world. For Heidegger man is not given in experience apart from the world: man's being (*Sein*) is only experienced as being-in-the-world (*in-der-Welt-sein*). Man is not isolated in his own subjectivity; he is there (*da*) where things are, in the midst of (*bei*) the things that make up the world. His being is then a *being there, Dasein,* and this is the curious name by which Heidegger chooses to identify the human being, or even *Da-sein,* to emphasize the human presence to things. It is almost impossible to overemphasize the importance of this concept and its linguistic ramifications (or the difficulty of trying to find an equivalent in English), and I will return to the term again and again in an effort to obtain a linguistic "fix" on the Heideggerian position. First, just a few words more on the relations between Heidegger's and Husserl's thought.

For Husserl, as we have seen, it is human consciousness that has absolute existence and that determines the meaning and being of all other things. Heidegger will go so far as to admit that the human being (*Da-sein*) has a certain indispensability as far as de-termining the "meaning of Being" (*der Sinn von Sein*) is concerned, that Being has meaning only so far as it "gets into" (*hereinsteht*) the understanding (*Verständlichkeit*) of *Dasein,*[57] a position not altogether remote from Husserl's, though it stresses dependence on man for the meaning or sense of Being (*Sinn von Sein*) rather than for Being

---

56. Spiegelberg, *The Phenomenological Movement,* p. 290.
57. Ibid., p. 285.

itself. As Magda King notes, " '*Sinn*' for Heidegger means that from which something is understandable as the thing it is."[58] Since it is only within human understanding that Being can be understood, it should not be stretching Heidegger's position to conclude that for him the "sense or meaning or Being" is dependent on the human being.[59]

Since, in any case, man is the only entity capable of knowing Being and concerned about (*umgegangen*) Being, it is entirely legitimate, and even necessary, to approach Being (*Sein*) by way of *Dasein*, and this is exactly the task which Heidegger sets himself in *Sein und Zeit*. This will not be an exploration of consciousness based upon a "bracketing" of the reality of everything else, in the manner of Husserlian "reduction," but an excursion into the meaning of Being, the reality of which can never for an instant be "bracketed" or set aside. In consequence, what we have in *Sein und Zeit* is not a transcendental phenomenology but an elementary ontology (*fundamentale Ontologie*). The method of the analysis, on the other hand, Heidegger (with a nod to Husserl) maintains, is phenomenological, but it is a *hermeneutic* rather than a transcendental phenomenology that is exemplified. "Hermeneutic" (from the Greek for "interpretive") is a standard term in Biblical theology, a term with which Heidegger must have been thoroughly acquainted from his days as a Jesuit seminarian. It conveys here the idea of *clarification of the meaning present.* This is a task analogous to that of Biblical *exegesis,* a leading out of the reality that is already there. It is an eduction, not a deduction or inference; an exegesis, not an *eisegesis* or "reading into" the experience as given. From a psychological perspective such a phenomenology would seem to remain closer to the psychological experience exactly as it occurs than does the *epoche* or reduction of Husserl but, as we shall see, hermeneutic phenomenology is far more than simple description, introspective

58. Magda King, *Heidegger's Philosophy* (New York: Macmillan, 1964), p. 6.

59. In many expositions of this doctrine there seems to be a subtle but momentous shift from the notion of human understanding as "that from which Being is *understood*" to "that from which Being is *understandable*" which seems very close to Husserl, though Heidegger flatly denies that human understanding determines the Being of things.

or behavioral.[60] Heidegger's *fundamental ontology* also has important psychological implications worthy of repeated consideration. I will deal with several of these in the course of developing an elementary glossary of Heideggerian terms.

It is Heidegger's general methodology (*Hermeneutike*) and his theory of human being (*Dasein*) that are the foci of Boss's *Daseinsanalyse*, the *existential analysis* which he offers as the most acceptable alternative to psychoanalysis and which he sees as providing a logically and experientially valid foundation for the two great scientific arts of medicine and psychology. We may now turn our attention to the transformation of psychoanalysis in the light of Heidegger's philosophy.

60. In his preface to William Richardson's comprehensive volume, *Heidegger: Through Phenomenology to Thought*, Heidegger, writing in 1962, still thinks that his view of the phenomenological method "as the process of letting things manifest themselves" (*Phänomenologie als das Sichzeigenlassen der Sache selbst*) is more faithful to the principle of phenomenology, which Husserl himself announced as *zu den Sachen selbst* ("Back to the things themselves"), than is Husserl's own *epoche*.

2

From Psychoanalysis
to Dasein-Analysis

The Transliteration
of *Daseinsanalyse*

In the Introduction I mentioned Boss's many years of
study in psychoanalysis and his eventual disillusionment with the
Freudian approach to the understanding and rectification of the
human condition. I also mentioned his immediate fascination with
the ideas of Heidegger, with which he first became acquainted
during World War II. Given the examples of Karl Jaspers and
Ludwig Binswanger, we can hardly say that the philosophically
oriented psychiatrist was quite the anomaly in the German-speaking world that he would have been in Britain or the United States.
It was, nevertheless, highly unusual for a middle-aged medical
practitioner to take up so refined and abstruse a philosophical system as Heidegger's and to make the mastery of that system his primary intellectual goal, a task that commanded the bulk of his time
for at least five years. It should be clear that this was in no sense a
career change since Boss continued to practice psychiatry as much
as possible during his years of study with Heidegger. On the contrary, Boss persevered in his extraordinarily demanding task precisely because he saw Heidegger's principles (both methodological
and substantive) as potentially having valuable applications in psychopathology and psychotherapy.

On the substantive level, Boss seems to have resonated particularly to Heidegger's *fundamentale Ontologie* of human being (*Dasein*)
as a meaning-disclosing openness to all reality (including itself), a
position to which we shall return shortly. He was, however,
equally impressed by Heidegger's phenomenological method of

attempting to understand human existence by the exclusive adher-
ence to what is given of it in direct experience, without the postu-
lation of forms or forces or structures or mechanisms derived from
sources external to direct human experience, postulations of the
kind that Boss saw increasingly as the root-evil in the Freudian and
all similar approaches. Because of its concentration on human existence, Heidegger's thought is sometimes regarded as a species of
existentialism, an attribution which Heidegger rejects because of
the connection of existentialism with the French philosophy of pessimism, atheism, and exclusive preoccupation with the human
condition. Also, while Heidegger acknowledges his own use of
phenomenology as a method, and his debt to Husserl for it, he has
refused to classify himself as a philosophical phenomenologist,
partly, no doubt, because phenomenology represents only an aspect of his thought and one that he no longer stresses, but mostly
perhaps because he did not see himself as a representative of any
school. He did not, indeed, even like to consider himself a philosopher, describing his profession not as philosophy but as
"thinking about Being" (*Denken des Seins*).[1] He was quite willing,
nonetheless, to accept Boss's term (borrowed from Binswanger)
for his modification of psychoanalysis, *Daseinsanalyse.* Unfortunately, this term, descriptive though it is in German, presents
some problems when we attempt to transliterate it into English.
The translation of Boss's first book on this subject was given the
title *Psychoanalysis and Daseinsanalysis.* This, like many other aspects
of that translation, was unfortunate. The second *s* in the German
Daseinsanalyse makes sense as indicating the genitive form, "the
analysis *of* Dasein," but there is no sense whatever in "Dasein-
analysis," which is neither English nor German. In transliterat-
ing, therefore, we would do better to drop the German genitive *s*
and substitute a hyphen for it: "Dasein-analysis." I will concede
that "Dasein-analysis" is not an especially graceful or memorable
term in English. If the accent is placed, as would be normal in
English, on the second syllable of *Dasein,* the whole term sounds
like "design-analysis" which, by analogy perhaps with "design

1. Martin Heidegger, "Brief Uber den Humanismus," in *Gesamtausgabe,* Band
9, *Wegmarken* (1936; Frankfurt: Klostermann, 1976), pp. 314-15, 364.

methods," suggests architectural theory rather than psychology; while the preferred pronunciation, "DAH-zine analysis," at best sounds very un-English and even more un-American. Perhaps the simplest solution for American psychologists and psychiatrists (who are unlikely to share Heidegger's historical and epistemological concerns) would be to translate *Daseinsanalyse* as "existential analysis" and the cognate psychological theory as "existential psychology," or, if they can tolerate an over-freighted term, "existential-phenomenological psychology," or, better perhaps, "phenomenological-existential psychology."

To understand Dasein-analysis we must understand Heidegger, at least in those respects in which his thought bears on what we in the United States would call "personality theory and psychotherapy," the general areas underlying the clinical understanding of human beings. Here Heidegger's language does present a problem, not only because he writes in a linguistically erudite German, very different from the academically technical language of a Wundt or a Külpe, but because it is a German that mixes so many styles, the philosophical and the popular, the historical and the current, the poetic and the pedestrian. Everyday terms are endowed with new and special meanings, often justified by elaborate analyses of Latin, Greek, and Germanic root forms, and it is easy to understand the belief that this Heideggerian metalanguage defies translation into an English that can be understood by clinicians with little background in philosophy or philology. However rashly, the present effort is predicated on the assumption that such translation is possible and can actually be accomplished with regard to the basic terminology of Heidegger's master work *Sein und Zeit*.[2] There are two considerations, I believe, that facilitate this work of translation. One is the relatively small number of novel terms involved, certainly fewer than sixty. The second is Heidegger's tendency to use each of these terms repeatedly in an increasingly

2. The metaphorical, poetic, and speculatively linguistic side of Heidegger increasingly dominates his writings after 1935, but these represent philosophical refinements of, rather than substantive changes in, the basic insights regarding human nature and hermeneutic methodology set forth in *Sein und Zeit*. We shall confine ourselves pretty much to the latter.

complex and varied series of combinations, almost like a musical theme-and-variations. Formal definitions in *Sein und Zeit* are rare, but many terms are exemplified so profusely that their meaning becomes eventually almost overwhelmingly clear. Once its novelty is recognized, Heidegger's language appears neither vague nor loose but very considered and consistent, often striking and memorable.

In what follows I will first attempt to explain the meaning-in-context of what I regard as the major terms of the Heidegger-Boss scheme and the theory of human being and human function that develops around them. In a final section I will analyze briefly how Freud offended against the first principle of hermeneutic phenomenology in seeking a physicalistic model for his theory of human motivation; and I will then from a critical-phenomenological perspective analyze the logical embarrassments to which two very different theories, 1) behavioristic reductionism and 2) the quasi phenomenological self theory of Carl Rogers, inevitably lead. I will deal finally with the strange confusions generated by the absence of phenomenological precision in developing neuropsychological explanations of experimental data.

The Terminology of Dasein-Analysis

The meaning of DASEIN. Though an acceptable English equivalent for *Dasein* has not been agreed to, the term is certainly not untranslatable. Literally "to be there" or "being there," *Dasein* in the ordinary German of the educated person means "being present" or "enduring" or "continuing to exist." Thus the Darwinian struggle for continued existence in German is *der Kampf ums Dasein*. The notion of "persisting through time" is certainly important to Heidegger's conception of human existence and undoubtedly a factor in his choice of the term, but there is more to his use of *Dasein* than this. Indeed, Heidegger seems to have taken advantage of the diffuse aura of the adverb *da* to convey something of the rich complexity of human existence. *Da* has a variety of implications and configural nuances that its English cognate "there" cannot begin to suggest: thus *dabei* (close to, at the same time, on hand), *darüber* (over it, concerning that, in the meantime), *dagegen* (on the contrary, in exchange for, in objection to), *daher* (thence, hence, along), *daselbst* (in that very place), and many more. When combined with the infinitive "to be" (*sein*), *da* suggests something like what we mean in English by being *with* something, as when we say "Get *with* it," i.e., "Be aware of the situation you're in and of your role in that situation and act accordingly." Throughout *Sein und Zeit* Heidegger seems to be saying that this is precisely the way in which the human being, as distinct from all other kinds of being, naturally is. Man is *with it* (*da*) in a way that no other entity is. It is a way of being aware of whatever comes into his experience and at the same time being aware of himself as a developing entity. *Dasein,* as the uniquely human mode of existence, is openness to all things, including itself. "Openness" (*Offenheit*) in this context means *openness to meaning,* and this, for Heidegger, is not a quality *of* a substance or object. Indeed, openness to meaning *is* human being, which Heidegger sees not as a static entity but as an act, a process. It is the very essence of human being to be open (= *Dasein*) to all things, including itself (which Heidegger calls "world openness," *Weltoffenheit*). We could therefore translate *Dasein* as "open being," but if we wish to stress its processive rather than substantive nature and to emphasize its uniquely human character of self-awareness, we might prefer the translation of *Dasein* as "human presence," for the human being is present to itself and to whatever comes within its range of awareness. Such "being present" is not a characteristic or attribute ascribed or added to human being; it *is* human being. Thus when Heidegger affirms the existentialist formula "Man's essence is his existence," he is saying simply that it is the nature of the human to "stand outside" (*ek-sistere*), so that it not only grasps the meaning of whatever comes into the range of its awareness in its vital contact with the world, but in doing so transcends the limitations of the present situation and projects itself toward the future and its own not-yet-fulfilled possibilities. It is man's meaning-illuminating and self-anticipatory *manner of being* that is unique and that justifies the attribution of the term "existence" ("standing outside itself") exclusively to him. Man's self-awareness, further, is not limited either to that segment of the material world constituted by his organism or to the actual state of his more-than-physical reality, but embraces his as yet unfulfilled possibilities, his own existence as "always able to be more." This was advanced by Heidegger not as a theory of man but as a hermeneutic unveiling of what is given in our immediate experience. Each of us has a direct awareness that to be human is to be open, to be self-transparently meaning-disclosing. *Human being is open being.*

Any translation of *Dasein* which stresses the notion of human existence or personal existence (Grene) cannot be said to be inaccurate, but it may not be very informative or specifically revealing of Heidegger's conception of the human condition. On the other hand, talking about *Dasein* as meaning "historical self-understanding of human being" (Schrag) seems more like an explanation than a translation, and a rather narrow one at that ("self-understanding"), since Heidegger stresses that *Dasein* is by nature open to understanding whatever comes into its presence ("being there") and not just open to itself. Also reading like a disquisition rather than a definition is Langan's "the human existence whose 'being there' forms a world within which there can be something," as well as Willliam Richardson's obliquely insightful "man's presence to the mystery of Presence." Such expansions of the meaning of the term are often interpretively helpful but they lack the compactness of an English term that translates a German term, as I believe "being present" or "human presence" translates *Dasein* as Heidegger uses the term in *Sein und Zeit.*[3]

The meaning of SEIENDE(S). The term *das Seiende* or *ein Seindes* is derived from the present participle (*seiend*) of the verb "to be" (*sein*). *Seiende(s)*, which in German is never plural, suggests "something that is" or for Heidegger "something that manifests Being." The German noun which is customarily translated "being" is not *das Seiende* but *das Sein*, which is, of course, derived from the infinitive "to be" (*sein*). To Heidegger *das Sein* is never *a* being but stands for the Being that all things share and manifest. I will endeavor to convey this restriction in English by using the capitalized "Being"

3. For informed and critical discussion of the condition, functions, and implications of *Dasein*, one may consult: Marjorie Grene, *Martin Heidegger* (New York: Hillary House, 1957); Calvin Schrag, *Existence and Freedom* (Evanston: Northwestern University Press, 1961); Thomas Langan, *The Meaning of Heidegger* (London: Routledge and Kegan Paul, 1959); William Richardson, *Heidegger: From Phenomenology to Thought*, 3rd ed. (The Hague: Nijhoff, 1974).

to translate *das Sein* and by avoiding as far as possible this form in the plural or with the indefinite article "a."

Regarding *Seiende(s)*, the German poses a difficulty since this term itself, as noted, is never used in the plural, though its context frequently suggests the plural.[4] Fortunately, English can convey the contextual plural of *Seiende(s)* when this is appropriate. When *Seiende(s)* is in context singular, the suggested translation is "the entity" or "an entity," or "a being" rather than "the being" or "being," in order to prevent confusion with "Being" (*das Sein*). Thus when Heidegger says, "Ontological interpretation . . . understands human openness or presence (*das Dasein*) and discovers it as *Seiendes* within the world" (*SuZ*, 130),[5] the sense of *Seiendes* seems to me to be singular and rendered nicely by "an entity"; but when in the same paragraph he refers to "the Being (*das Sein*) of the *Seienden* there with us," the term *Seienden* (genitive case) is contextually plural and can best be conveyed by the English "of the entities" or (my hesitant second choice) "of the beings." For a similar reason, in the plural context "entities" would seem to be a better translation than "existents" since the latter term suggests and sounds like "existence," which is the obvious translation of Heidegger's *Existenz*, a term reserved for the unique mode of human being (*die Seinsart des Daseins*) and an entirely different term from *Seiende(s)*, which applies to much besides human being. Accordingly, when the context suggests the singular, I prefer to translate *das Seiende* by "the entity" and *ein Seiendes* by "an entity" (or possibly "a being"), and when the context suggests the plural, by "the entities" or "the beings." For Heidegger it is important that the plural instances of *Seiende(s)* always be distinguished from the Being (*das Sein*) that they manifest, and this is one major reason for preferring the translation in the plural as "entities" rather than "beings," though the latter must be regarded as acceptable, if less

4. If it were *das Sein* that was never pluralized, it would suit Heidegger's thought perfectly, but in this respect his beloved German seems to have let him down, since *Seiende(s)* which may be ontologically plural is always grammatically singular, while *Sein* which is ontologically one need not remain grammatically singular!

5. *SuZ* is the abbreviation I will use for the German text of *Sein und Zeit,* and the accompanying number corresponds to the page of the original edition (1927) of Heidegger's master work.

clear. Heidegger insists that what he calls "Being" is not an entity but that which determines every entity as an entity (*SuZ*, 6); while an entity (*ein Seiendes*) is anything that *is*, be it actual like my own vocation as a university professor, or possible like my still unfulfilled possibilities of existence (*Seinkönnen*), e.g., my being the author of this monograph when it is finished; concrete like *this dog* or *that dress*, or abstract like *justice* and *beauty;* tangible like *female* or *table*, or impalpable like *awareness* or *evaluated meaning*. Examples of non-*Seiendes* are those conditions that are necessary to provide a baseline or "horizon" for *Seiendes* to exist and function, especially for the *Seiende* we call *Dasein*. Thus *temporality* is the meaning of the Being of *Dasein*, but *Zeitlichkeit* is not itself an entity (*Seiendes*); and the *world* (*die Welt*) is the necessary horizon of the human entity, which can exist only as being-in-the-world (*in-der-Welt-sein*), yet the world is not itself a *Seiendes* but the common sphere of activity pertaining to but not constituted by all the *Seiende* (people, their beliefs, values, interests, their possessions, instruments, gear, and structures) involved in it.

The meaning of MITSEIN. Sometimes written with a hyphen (*Mit-sein*) or even as *Miteinandersein* ("to-be-with-one-another") to emphasize the reciprocal nature of the relation between people, *Mit-sein* conveys the essential interdependence of human beings; not spatial or temporal togetherness, but the being together of two entities each of whom is aware of itself and the other and of their essential similarity or community. I therefore translate *Mitsein* as "human togetherness" and note that for Heidegger and Boss animals cannot be together in the sense of *Mitsein*. Human togetherness in this sense is not a contingent situation that may in certain circumstances be lacking, but denotes a primary mode of human being in the absence of which there would be nothing that we could recognize as human life.[6] Together human beings sustain and maintain their common world by their receptive presence or openness to whatever manifests itself to them, and this "whatever" very importantly includes "each other." It is this shared presence or openness, which Heidegger contends is immediately recognized

---

6. *Mitdasein* means something different, viz., any person other than I. *Mitsein* is an *existentiale* or *existential prerequisite*, something without which no human being or *Dasein* can be. *Mitdasein* is simply the other person, as distinct from me.

by everyone, that is the sign of their common humanity. The "clearing" (*Lichtung*) in which things can be perceived and related to is a common rather than a purely individual enterprise. One cannot live in the world without living *with* other people: to exist as a human being is to coexist.

It is worth repeating that the *world* for Heidegger and Boss is not the section of the physical cosmos in which we happen to be situated; it is not even the totality of that cosmos. Our world is the human world, incorporating primarily (but not exclusively) human entities—that *Seiende* other than the subject ("I") that we call *Mitdasein*—and including all that is useful (*zuhanden*) for human life, the "equipment" (*Zeug*) that we need to survive and flourish as human beings. It is in this sense of "world" that "to-be-in-the-world" (*in-der-Welt-sein*) is part and parcel of our very essence as human, an *Existenzial* in its own right.

Twentieth-century social science has placed great stress on the almost total dependence of human existence on other humans and the consequent shaping of human attitude and behavior by the group. Social scientists have thus argued tellingly that the individual human perceives "reality" (including his own actions) from the perspective of socially determined biases; that the meaning of events is construed according to sociocultural criteria. The common humanity that unites us is not, as the British empiricists and the philosophers of the Enlightenment imagined, first recognized in ourselves and then in comparing others with our own humanity. Rather, our contemporaries would say, we come to recognize our own humanity bit by bit through the communication to us of the perceptions of others. Even our self-concept, as Sullivan and Mead argue, is basically composed of the "reflected appraisals of significant others." Philosophically, Heidegger recognizes all this perfectly, even arguing that these facts are ontologically rooted in the nature of human existence. By nature man is "thrown" (*geworfen*) into a world whose character he does not determine but which does much to determine his. In his helpless dependency the human being necessarily "falls victim" (a process which Heidegger calls *Verfallensein*) to the values and attitudes of others or, better, *the Other* (*das Man*), a noun formed from the indefinite personal pronoun *man* and having no precise equivalent in English, though approximated by "the They" and "the Other." The

German *man* is used much more than the English "one," which is
correct but seldom employed in ordinary conversation. Where the
German says "one sees with the eyes" (*Man sieht mit den Augen*), we
would say in everyday English "We see with our eyes" or "You
see with your eyes." Interestingly, English popular usage under-
scores the point made by Heidegger that the pseudo-personal
"one" (*man*) all too easily becomes "you" or "we." When we tell
young people " *You* don't behave that way in public" or " *We* don't
use that kind of language here," we are telling them in effect that
the individual's very self is not his to live free with but must exhibit
the conduct and exemplify the values approved by the group. This
self-as-dictated-by-others is what Heidegger calls the *Man-selbst,*
which is not totally remote from what Erich Fromm meant by the
"other-directed man." And for Heidegger the phenomenon is
more deeply revealing and pervasive than it is for, say, Fromm or
Riesman since it is founded on the very nature of the human
being, "thrown" into the world and "fallen prey" to it. Thus this
is not a condition that human beings can help or for which they can
be criticized, but one that pertains to their very essence as human.[7]

Mitsein therefore represents a kind of dilution of the individuality of *Dasein.* The individual is so absorbed in and by the world
that he is distracted from the being that is his alone to appreciate,
and is in a state of "unmindfulness of Being" (*Seinsvergessenheit*), a
condition that happens inevitably to every one of us.

But, Heidegger adds, this is not all there is to the human being.
There is in human "being present" (*Dasein*) an awareness of its
own nature as *ek-sistent,* as standing outside of the present moment
and seeing the future possibilities which are its own. The human
being is thus not only forfeit or prey to the world and "the Other"
(*verfallen in das Man*), but also transcendent thereof, at least potentially, in its ability to project (*entwerfen*) its future possibilities. How
Dasein is able to realize these possibilities is in Heidegger a complicated story to which we will shortly return.

The meaning of ZEITLICHKEIT. Since the notion of time is already

7. See the section on Sullivan in Joseph F. Rychlak, *Introduction to Personality and
Psychotherapy,* 2nd ed. (Boston: Houghton Mifflin, 1981); also George H. Mead,
Mind, Self, and Society (Chicago: University of Chicago Press, 1934); Erich Fromm,
Man for Himself (New York: Rinehart, 1947); David Riesman, *The Lonely Crowd*
(New Haven: Yale University Press, 1950).

abstract, "temporality" might seem to be an abstraction of an abstraction; nevertheless, as used by Heidegger and Boss, temporality is far less remote and dehumanized than the conception of time common in the physical sciences. To Heidegger time is neither an infinite series of instants or "now-points" (*Jetztpunkte*) nor a kind of spatialized container in which things are, but the horizon or background or setting for all understanding and interpretation of Being. In particular, says *Sein und Zeit* (17), *temporality is the meaning of the Being of Dasein*. From his past-determined *thrownness*, which is that about man that is least his own since it is given to him by the physical and social forces that have originated him; to that future condition which is most man's own—"his ownmost possibility of Being" (*sein eigenstes Seinkönnen*), as Heidegger puts it— viz., his death;[8] to the everyday now with which man is necessarily so preoccupied that he tends to be oblivious of the very Being that is his to fulfill (*Seinsvergessenheit*), a preoccupation he must transcend if he is to attain authenticity (*Eigentlichkeit*), the human being is always defined by the temporal conditions that subtend his every act.

It would seem to follow that temporality in this sense is a human attribute. Grene conveys this sense by translating *Zeitlichkeit* as "personal time," which seems to overlook the difference between *Zeit* and *Zeitlichkeit* but may still agree with Heidegger, whom I understand as indicating that *Zeitlichkeit* is the human quality of being temporal or "human temporality." The time to which this temporality refers is, then, not something *in* which we are but the very *way* we are. By the same token, we can agree with Boss that phenomenologically we can be said to "have time" only in the sense that we *are temporal;* just as we have concern in the sense that we are concerned, or have anxiety in the sense that we are anxious. There is therefore no implication that time or temporality has any existence apart from the human condition, any more than concern or anxiety has.

We may say therefore that our human presence (*Dasein*) is always temporally disposed, that we are attuned to the whole range of time so that we are aware not only of what is momentarily

8. Heidegger sees death as the one experience impossible to share, since each of us must die entirely alone.

present but of what has been and of what can be or is to come. To be human, then, is to be aware of the present and retentive of the past and, above all, anticipatory of the future, and all of these simultaneously. This is time not as abstracted from cosmic motion but as we experience it, time as lived phenomenon rather than as hypothesized noumenon. It is in this sense that being temporal is the meaning of our Being, that from which our Being is understandable as the thing it is, and the closest correlative of Being (*Sein*) is Time (*Zeit*); hence the title of Heidegger's *Meisterwerk, Sein und Zeit.*

To Boss time as we experience it is always *teleological* or purpose-oriented; time for something humanly useful (*zuhanden*) or for some interpersonal exchange. Personal time is also always related to human events, individual or social, for example, *now* as I write these words or the effort to revive the disarmament negotiations proceeds; *then* when we first met or the war was still on; or *later* when I've finished this research or when peace has been restored in the Middle East. In this human perspective time is more than Aristotle's "measure of motion according to a before and after," and is to be construed not as a mere metric of inanimate movement but as a dating of human events according to some kind of succession. This succession, Boss would further insist, is not a purely subjective experience or private intuition of "now" or "earlier" or "later," but an experience to be shared with and communicated to others. Finally, far from being a series of discrete moments or "now-points," time as experienced is a continuing duration or extension (*Geweitetheit*) whose "now" is continuous and integral with its "then" and directed toward its future "when." Thus the "now" that we experience is not an instant but a period of time, a duration or extent, such as a half-hour's conversation or an evening's entertainment. The physicist, using the infinitesimal calculus, may find it convenient to look at time as though it were a series of discrete and infinitesimal instants, but that does not alter the reality of what we experience, and it is this latter with which, say Heidegger and Boss, we must begin our reflections concerning the real nature of time in human life.[9]

9. Medard Boss, *Existential Foundations of Medicine and Psychology* (New York: Jason Aronson, 1979).

We should note also that since the time with which Heidegger and Boss are concerned is that in which human life is lived, time is essentially finite or limited, having, like human life itself, a necessary beginning and an inevitable ending. Finitude is therefore of the essence of time as we experience it.

The meaning of BEFINDLICHKEIT *and its distinction from* VERSTEHEN. In German the verb *sich befinden* (literally, to find itself, that is, be situated), like the French *se trouver,* can be used to denote the location or situation of anything. Heidegger and Boss, however, do not use the reflexive form *sich befinden* to designate the situation or location of nonhuman beings, but only the individual human's self-disclosing set toward his or her own situation. *Befindlichkeit*—the abstract, rather archaic form suggesting something like "situatedness"—is personalized, and somewhat concretized, by Heidegger and Boss, as an orienting attitude of the individual toward his actual situation. It is important to note this last point since Heidegger distinguishes *Befindlichkeit* from that special kind of "understanding" (*Verstehen*) that denotes *appreciation of the possible;* thus *Befindlichkeit* is primarily concerned with the actual, not with what man can be but how he finds himself (*sich befinden*) in fact to be. Thus our stance toward our "thrownness" is *Befindlichkeit,* as is our posture toward the fact of our Being-in-the-world (*in-der-Welt-sein*) (*SuZ,* 143).

Again, one should not make the mistake of supposing that *Befindlichkeit* is a feeling which happens to come over us at times, since it is a primordial characteristic of *Dasein* with reference to all its actual states of being such as "thrownness," being concerned (*umgegangen*) with the world, our "fallenness" (*Verfallenheit*), and the like.

Macquarrie and Robinson's translation of *Befindlichkeit* as "state of mind" seems singularly inept and un-Heideggerian, as well as being so vague and generic as to apply to every cognitive or appetitive condition from a reverence for eternal beauty to political conviction or hypochondria.[10] In its colloquial meaning also, "state of mind" is like "mood" and connotes generally a temporary condition, an attitude that is essentially particular rather than (as Heidegger sees it) something that is part of the ontological structure of

10. Boss, *Psychoanalysis and Daseinsanalysis,* trans. Lefebre.

Dasein, an *existentiale* or necessary prerequisite of human existence. One might therefore propose the translation of *Befindlichkeit* as "self-orienting attitude" or "self-disclosing attitude," and add its reference to "the actual situation in which one finds oneself." Simplest of all perhaps, yet quite comprehensive withal, would be the translation of *Befindlichkeit* as "the sense of one's actual situation." We could then translate *Verstehen* in context (*SuZ,* 143) as "appreciation of the possible." Where necessary to distinguish this use of *Verstehen* from its ordinary sense of "understanding" in Heidegger we might say "primordial understanding" or "primordial appreciation" or "understanding as an existential prerequisite (*existentiale*)." The contrast between "the sense of one's actual situation" and "the appreciation of one's possibilities" seems in accord with common sense as well as with decent English usage.

The meaning of DIE ANGST. The usual translation of *die Angst* as "anxiety" is in certain respects too general, in others too specific, to express with reasonable closeness what Heidegger seems to mean by this term. "Anxiety" to psychologists and psychiatrists is likely to have primary reference to psychopathological phenomena, as in "neurotic anxiety," "free-floating anxiety," "defenses against anxiety," and the like. One element common to psychopathological anxiety and Heidegger's notion of *Angst* (which Boss seems to apply without much modification to psychiatry) is the indefinite or indeterminate (*unbestimmt*) nature of its object. But far from being abnormal, Heidegger's *Angst* is a basic and universal self-disclosing attitude (*Befindlichkeit*) proper to the human condition. *Die Angst,* says Heidegger, "is one of *Dasein*'s possibilities[11] of Being and together with *Dasein* itself as disclosed in it provides the phenomenal basis for the explicit grasp of the primordial totality of the Being of *Dasein*" (*SuZ,* 182).

Nor is *Angst* well translated by "anguish," however apt the latter term may be for conveying the despair and painful wretchedness that certain existentialists see as characterizing man's lot. In English, "anguish" seems to designate most clearly an intense form of grief or painful loss in its physical as well as its psychic as-

11. Does Heidegger slip here by referring to a *Befindlichkeit* as a possibility (*Möglichkeit*)?

pects, a kind of psychophysical agony, which is far from the contextual sense of Heidegger's *Angst.*

There may be much less to object to in the term "dread" as a fair rendering of *Angst* in Heidegger. There is some precedent too in that "dread" is often used to translate *Angst* in Kierkegaard, and Heidegger certainly admired and borrowed freely from Kierkegaard's views on this phenomenon. Kierkegaard's *Angst,* like Heidegger's, lacks a definite object, though indefiniteness is not intrinsic to the meaning of "dread" in English.[12] (One may thus dread an ordeal, the full scope and detail of which he understands all too clearly.) If the term "dread" then catches something characteristic of Heidegger's *Angst,* it still omits the important quality of indefiniteness or indeterminateness (which a term like "anxiety" usually has and terms like "dismay" and "apprehension," it seems to me, at least suggest). I suppose one could say "generalized dread" or "indeterminate dread," though the former seems somewhat ambiguous and the latter suggests that the state rather than its object is indeterminate.

To understand *in context* Heidegger's sense of *Angst,* we may recall that for Heidegger human existence as such is subordinated to a "world" which it encounters, and this subordination (*Angewiesenheit*) is part and parcel of its very Being: "*zu seinem Sein gehört wesenhaft diese Angewiesenheit*" (*SuZ,* 87). In other words, this world and its many features are not of the individual's doing but something in the midst of which he is "thrown" (*geworfen*) and to which he is "fallen victim" (*verfallen*) or, in Karl Rahner's term, "enslaved." The human being naturally shrinks from this victimization or enslavement by the world, and this is one basis of *Angst.*[13]

For Heidegger, too, it is a strange world to us and bound to give rise to a sense of total unfamiliarity or *uncanniness* (*Unheimlichkeit*). Yet "Being-in-the-world" is a basic condition of human existence so that, in shrinking back from the world, *Dasein* is shrinking back from itself or at least from an essential aspect of itself. This is not *fear* (*Furcht*) in the ordinary sense because its object is no concrete

12. Martin Heidegger, *Was heisst Denken?* (Tübingen: Niemeyer, 1954).

13. One thinks of Housman's *Shropshire Lad:* "I a stranger and afraid / In a world I never made."

thing nor anything practicable (*zuhanden*). In *Angst* that about which we are uneasy is not nothing (*totales Nichts*), but it is nowhere (*nirgends*) and the threat which it connotes is quite indefinite (*unbestimmt*). One turns away from the world in an attitude of general apprehensiveness and uncertainty about one's ability to cope with the world, combined with a sense of alienation, of not being at home (*Heim*) in the world, a feeling that amounts to "uncanniness" (*Unheimlichkeit*). Perhaps also, though this is not entirely clear, when we are oriented toward the actuality of our being in the world, we divine that we were not always there and will not always be there, that our sojourn in the world is a present condition bounded on both sides, past and future, by *nothingness* (*Nichtigkeit*). What emerges from this is not the ordinary fear of dying, but the powerful and yet vague uneasiness at the inevitability of our nonexistence, our ceasing to be. This latter, too, is a kind of *Nichts* (nothing) or *Nichtigkeit* (nothingness) and would seem to play a key part in the emergence of *die Angst* as a basic self-orienting attitude (*Grundbefindlichkeit*). *Angst,* indeed, seems caught between the Scylla of "thrownness and enslavement in the world" and the Charybdis of "ceasing to be altogether." I believe that the translation of *die Angst* should reflect both uncanniness and inability to cope, on the one hand, and uneasiness at the prospect of annihilation on the other, and I suggest, more or less in the order of preference, "dismayed apprehensiveness," "anxious uncertainty," or "dismayed foreboding."[14]

On the positive side, we should note that for Heidegger *die Angst* throws human existence back on itself, at least briefly isolates (*vereinzelt*) man from other things in the world, and thereby makes him focus on his own possibilities and the freedom to develop these possibilities which is his. Until the shock of *Angst* jars him out of his

14. The term "existential anxiety" may also have some claim to validity as a translation of *die Angst* in Heidegger, since the underlying attitude (*Befindlichkeit*) is concerned with existence (and its opposite), and the term "anxiety" includes the element of indefiniteness as well as fearfulness in its connotation. My chief objection to this translation is that "existential" and "existence" are well-known Heideggerian terms having a distinctive significance quite different from that involved in translating *die Angst* as "existential anxiety" or "anxiety regarding existence," which would make this way of translating the term more confusing than clarifying.

state of fallenness (*Verfallenheit*) and unmindfulness of Being (*Seins-vergessenheit*), man cannot begin to strive for authenticity.

The meaning of VORHANDEN *and* ZUHANDEN. The terms *vorhanden* and *zuhanden* are applied by Heidegger only to entities other than the human (*Dasein*). That which is *vorhanden* is simply present or on hand, and not contributory to any human purpose. When something is humanly useful, however, it becomes not merely an object of knowledge but an object of concern. It is then *zuhanden*. In human "spatialness" (*Räumlichkeit*), as we shall see, there may be recognition of some objects as merely present or "within range" without any implication of their having utility—sometimes, in fact, with the implication of their *not* being of value or of their interfering with the achievement of human goals, extreme instances of *not* being *zuhanden*, though certainly known to be present (*vorhanden*).

Lefebre, the translator of Boss's *Psychoanalysis and Daseinsanalysis*, accepts Lyons's suggestion to translate *vorhanden* by "extant," and regards this as preferable to other translations such as "on hand," "present," "before us," "present at hand," etc. Why one should prefer an unusual and, in part at least, obscure term like "extant" to a simple word like "present" is difficult to understand. The original meaning of "extant," according to Webster, is "standing out, hence conspicuous," which is certainly different from Heidegger's use of *vorhanden*, as is the current sense given to "extant" by Webster, viz., "still existing, not extinct."[15] As Lefebre acknowledges, "*vorhanden* is . . . used to refer 'to the world of objects present merely as such.' "[16] Why not then translate it by "simply present" or "merely present"?

The related term *zuhanden* Lefebre translates by "at hand," which fails utterly to convey the sense of usefulness or instrumentality essential in Heidegger's use of *zuhanden*. Even while recognizing the element of "instrumentality" as involved in *zuhanden*, Lefebre beclouds the issue by quoting approvingly the description of *zuhanden* by May, Angel, and Ellenberger in their volume *Exis-*

15. *Webster's New World Dictionary of the American Language*, college ed. (Cleveland: World Publishing, 1966).

16. Boss, *Psychoanalysis and Daseinsanalysis*, trans. Lefebre, p. 43, fn.

tence: " 'At hand' (*zuhanden*), the companion term to 'extant' (*vorhanden*), is used to refer to the world of human things, which are present as instrumentalities for existing beings.''[17] For Heidegger, as I have noted, the "things" referred to by *zuhanden* are never human beings, so to call them "human things" is at best confusing; on the other hand, the "existing beings" for whom these things are useful as instrumentalities are always human beings. So Lefebre's "human things" are not human and his "existing beings" are, a curious inversion in translation. At all odds, much of the confusion can be prevented if we translate *zuhanden* simply as "humanly useful."

These terms are extremely important because in Heidegger's view our most primordial relation with the things in the world is from the perspective of their utility. We first see things not as merely present (*vorhanden*) but as ready to use (*zuhanden*). As Grene notes, Heidegger sees man as *homo faber* before he is *homo sapiens.*[18] The disinterested contemplation of entities in the world, however dear to the heart of the philosophers and "pure" scientists among us, is to Heidegger a secondary and derivative attitude. We thus breathe the air before we analyze it, eat the food before we determine its caloric value, use the door latch before we wonder how it works, before we even become distinctly aware of it as something in itself, something that is just there (*vorhanden*).

The meaning of SORGE, BESORGEN, *and* FURSORGE. The most fundamental of these three related terms for Heidegger is *Sorge* literally "care," but in the context of *Sein und Zeit* having a far more complex and exact meaning). In Heidegger's view, indeed, *Sorge* is the very Being of *Dasein* (*Sein des Daseins*), bringing together its three primary modes of Being: 1) its *thrownness*, which Heidegger often refers to as its "facticity" (*Faktizität*), what it is "made" to be, and which embraces its attitude toward things in the world as useful (*zuhanden*); 2) its *existentiality* or transcendence (*Transzendenz*), its standing outside (*ek-sistere*) itself, so to say, in order to be in vital contact with the world and aware of itself and its possibilities to be fulfilled; and 3) its "victimization" (*Verfallensein*) or distraction by

17. Rollo May, Ernest Angel, and Henri F. Ellenberger, eds., *Existence* (New York: Basic Books, 1958), p. 276.
18. Grene, *Heidegger*, p. 22.

the entities (*Seiendes*) in the world and its obliviousness of Being (*Seinsvergessenheit*). Man is as necessarily involved in and concerned with the world and with his state in the world as he is with his own fulfilment. He is involved and committed as "thrown" (*geworfen*), as caught up (*verfallen*) in the everyday affairs of the world, and as transcendent (*ek-sisting*). This is what Heidegger means by *Sorge* in the context of *Sein und Zeit,* which I therefore translate as "involved commitment" or "committed involvement."

Looking at man as he is amid the environment (*Umwelt*) of useful things and the *Mitwelt* of other people, there are two experiential or "ontic" modes of *Sorge* which Heidegger calls *Besorgen* and *Fürsorge*. In the pages of *Sein und Zeit,* the neuter noun *das Besorgen* is always portrayed in relation to *things,* especially things which are humanly useful (*zuhanden*). Its phenomenological opposite would appear to be a carelessness (with tools and other useful possessions and facilities). I therefore translate *das Besorgen* as *carefulness* (with things) or *taking care of* (things). By contrast, *die Fürsorge* always relates to persons, to that particular kind of entity (*Seiendes*) which, or rather who, is never merely present (*vorhanden*) or useful (*zuhanden*), because it is not a thing to do with or merely note but a person to *be with* (*Mitsein*) and to care for. It is this caring for or concern for that is expressed by *Fürsorge,* which I accordingly translate as "concern for others."

Heidegger identifies a characteristic type of perception or "vision" (*Sicht*) for each of these modes of *Sorge*. For *Besorgen* there is *Umsicht* ("circumspection" or "looking around" or "looking over" the situation); for *Fürsorge* there is *Rücksicht* ("considerateness") or *Nachsicht* ("indulgence" or "looking after" others); and corresponding to the individual's involved commitment (*Sorge*) to his own being is the mode of perception that Heidegger calls *Durchsichtigkeit* ("transparency" or "looking into oneself," or, better, "looking *through* one's present self to one's future possibilities").

The meaning of GESTIMMTHEIT *and* STIMMUNG. The term *Gestimmtheit* (sometimes equated with, though not the same as, *Bestimmtheit*) has far greater generality in German than its literal translation in English ("attunement"), since *Gestimmtheit* is not limited to sound, but may be applied to light and color, emotions and motives, and to all manner of other things, including the weather! To convey anything of this generality in English we have to resort to a more abstract—perhaps too abstract—term, such as "disposition" or, possibly, "set." Apart from their abstractness or absence of "color," there are other difficulties with these words. The natural opposite to "disposition," viz., "indisposition," has a totally different usual meaning ("slight illness"), which also holds for its adjectival correlative, "indisposed." The term "set" has no corresponding adjective and no opposite, "unset" and "setless" being awkward to the point of silliness. The German adjectival forms (*ungestimmt* or *unbestimmt*) are, of course, regular and appropriate. This only makes greater the temptation to take the English word "attuned"—which has an acceptable, if hardly felicitous, opposite, "unattuned"—and stretch it in a manner analogous to the German. This is, however, a fatal temptation since in English we are sure to wind up (as does Lefebre in his translation of *Psychanalyse und Daseinsanalyse*) with hopelessly mixed metaphors like the "attunement of the light" and the "unattuned being there" (*ungestimmtes Dasein*), which simply won't wash. In our mother tongue, whatever its flexibility, a light cannot be "tuned" or "toned," but it can be set or adjusted or, in general, *disposed* in a variety of ways, as may an attitude or a motive or a number of other mental states.

Some might opt for the word "set" as a translation for *Gestimmtheit,* and I concede that in some contexts the English "set" comes close to conveying the sense of *Gestimmtheit.* But "set" in German is basically *Einstellung* (an important term in the experimental investigations of the Würzburg school), and the term, despite its currency and its respectable empirical history, seems never to have been used by Heidegger or Boss as equivalent to *Gestimmtheit.* "Disposition" and "disposed" are unquestionably less restrictive terms than "set" and can be appropriately negated by "indetermination" and "indeterminate" where "indisposition" or "indisposed" might be ambiguous or otherwise inappropiate. On these accounts, "disposition" would seem to deserve preference as the translation of *Gestimmtheit.*

The question remains as to how to translate the related term *Stimmung* (which in everyday German has a variety of meanings including "tune," "voice," "mood," and "state of mind") without mixing metaphors, succumbing to the fallacy of misplaced concreteness, or losing the legitimate generality of the notion as set forth by Heidegger. "Mood" does not seem to be a quite adequate rendering of *Stimmung* since "mood" suggests a temporary state, a transitory condition of a purely emotional nature. From the context of *Sein und Zeit* it would seem that *Stimmung* may be a quite sustained attitude (*Befindlichkeit*) and that it need not be purely emotional in reference (*SuZ*, 134), though in the Heidegger-Boss presentation it most often does relate to the emotional coloring of human activity and receptivity. In such contexts *Stimmung* might be most appropriately rendered by "emotional disposition," which would also indicte its relation to *Gestimmtheit* (translated simply as "disposition"). There are other contexts in Heidegger and Boss where "motivational disposition" or even "temperamental disposition" might be acceptable translations of *Stimmung*.

   The meaning of STERBEN *and* DER TOD. For Heidegger *sterben* ("to die") and *der Tod* ("death") are distinctively, indeed exclusively, human characteristics since only the human knows of the inevitability of his own ceasing-to-be-as-a-human-being. On this account, human existence never merely comes to an end ("to come to an end" is *verenden*, a term Heidegger never uses with regard to human dying). Phenomenologically, we learn about death through the repeated experience of the death of others, but the appreciation of the reality and certainty of our own death is an essential aspect of human self-transparent openness. In truth, you do not begin to live in human fashion until you are aware of the fact that in a certain sense you are dying! Not dying immediately, of course, but inevitably and very personally. Once we realize that we are to die, we are in a permanent relationship to death and our very existence is then *Sein-zum-Tode*, Being-unto-death or Being-toward-death. To be dying (*sterben*), says Heidegger (*SuZ*, 247), is not just something that happens to us, but that way of Being (*Seinsweise*) in which *Dasein* is toward its death. This is true even though the prospect of nonexistence is a terrifying one before which man shrinks and against which he, following the Other (*das Man*), defends himself by denial, diversion, and various other unrealistic maneuvers. This defensiveness, however, serves to mask the all-important truth that it is death that gives meaning to life. As Boss notes, man's actions are meaningful because each moment of life occurs only once and if man does not act to fulfill himself at that time, he must remain in some regard forever unfulfilled. Death, says

Heidegger, is a possibility of Being that human presence (*Dasein*) must always itself take over (*SuZ*, 250 ff.). With respect to death, *Dasein* stands before itself in that possibility of Being which in the highest degree is its very own (*mit dem Tod steht sich das Dasein selbst in seinem eigensten Seinkönnen bevor*). In this confrontration all relations to any other human entity are dissolved. Man faces death alone.

The human being must also regard the prospect of nonexistence with that dismayed apprehensiveness which Heidegger means by *die Angst*. This, of course, is not just fear (*Furcht*) of giving up life (*ableben*) but a basic self-disclosure (*Grundbefindlichkeit*) that our human existence is not only thrown (*geworfen*) into the world but thereby toward its own end (*Ende*) which is death. This is the dismayed apprehensiveness at the prospect of death (*die Angst vor dem Tode*), the natural accompaniment of man's recognition of his very Being-unto-death (*Sein-zum-Tode*). Naturally, it also prompts a flight (*Flucht*) from the "uncanniness" (*Unheimlichkeit*) of no-longer-being-able-to-be-as-human-presence (*Nicht-mehr-dasein-können*), a retreat to the popular illusion that death is "something that happens to others" and that there is no reason for you to be concerned with it now. Most important, it is also a retreat from oneself, from one's "ownmost Being-toward-death" (*das eigenste Sein-zum-Tode*), an ineffectual denial of the awareness of death as something that can happen to *me* at any instant and an event that gives definitive meaning to my life.

The meaning of GEWISSEN *and* SCHULD. As a derivative of the verb meaning "to know" (*wissen*), it is clear that *das Gewissen* (literally, "the conscience," which in English also implies a kind of knowledge) is not a blind grope but a kind of knowing urge, an at least subconscious registration of an ideal or value. It would seem further that to Heidegger the underlying and determinative reality is the unfinished or still-to-be-completed nature of human existence. At the same time, *Sein und Zeit* (269 ff.) does not present *das Gewissen* as a merely contemplative awareness of a remote ideal but as a concrete cognizance of the need to act in order to realize our possibilities. What *Gewissen* makes us aware of is our *debt* or guilt—the word *Schuld* means both—to Being. Thus *Schuld* and *Gewissen* are for Heidegger part of the structure of *Sorge* (involved commitment) which, we have seen, is the very Being of *Dasein*. And since *Dasein* is *always not yet* the fulfilled possibilities to which it is by nature committed, *Dasein* is by nature unfulfilled, which is "being guilty" (*Schuldigsein*) in Heidegger's "ontological" sense or, we might say, *responsible* for the fulfilment of its own possibilities.

What Heidegger then designates the "call of conscience" (*der Gewissensruf*) is the explicitly conscious self-disclosure (*Erschlossenheit*) of the commitment to self-realization which is contained in *Sorge*. This call summons *Dasein* to the fulfilment of its ownmost possibilities, but since *Sorge* is the very Being of *Dasein*, the summons in question is of *Dasein* to itself. Thrown into the world, the human being tends, as we have seen, to fall victim (*verfallen*) to the attitudes and beliefs of the "They" or the generalized Other (*das Man*) and to follow these blindly. But the recognition of the commitment to self-fulfilment can call it back to itself, and when it responds to this call, Heidegger maintains, there results a new and motivationally powerful mode of self-disclosedness (*Erschlossenheit*) which he calls *Entschlossenheit*, by which he seems to mean not only self-revelation but *self-affirmation*. This self-affirmation can anticipate both *Dasein*'s orientation toward death and toward the possibilities it is to fulfill in its life situation. It is the *anticipatory self-affirmation* (*vorlaufende Entschlossenheit*) that enables *Dasein* to achieve *authenticity* (*Eigentlichkeit*), i.e., the state of being fully aware of itself, its life situation, and its possibilities; and of moving realistically toward their realization, including especially that unique possibility of death, which gives finality and meaning to life as a whole.

The translations suggested by the context of these terms are as follows:

Term	Literal Meaning	Contextual Meaning
das Gewissen	the conscience	the thrust toward self-realization
der Gewissensruff	the call of conscience	the disclosure of the commitment to self-realization
Erschlossenheit	disclosedness	deliberate self-disclosure
Entschlossenheit	resolution, determination	deliberate self-affirmation
die Schuld	guilt, debt	the responsibility to realize one's possibilities

Though none of these terms for Heidegger is to be taken quite literally, the special meaning he gives these terms in *Sein und Zeit* denotes the ontological basis for their conventional meaning in human experience, namely, the moral phenomena of conscience and guilt, self-evaluation and resolution.

The meaning of LICHTUNG. Though cognate with the noun "light" (*das Licht*), the verb *lichten* and the noun derived from it, *die Lichtung,* ordinarily mean "to clear" and "clearing" (as in the woods) respectively, thus having only indirect reference to "light" (the verb) and "illumination" (which in ordinary German are *beleuchten* and *Beleuchtung,* respectively). This indirect reference is important to Heidegger's and Boss's thought, however, for "the clearing of Being" (*die Lichtung des Seins*) to which they refer is the openness of human presence itself (*Dasein*), which is "illuminated" (*erleuchtet*) and "cleared" (*gelichtet*) not through any other entity, but in such a fashion that it is itself the clearing (*SuZ,* 133). Popular thought refers to a natural light (*lumen naturale*) in man, but in a deeper sense the clearing is not in man; rather, it *is* man. And it is in this clearing that the things encountered in the world are "brought to light" and their meaning understood.

The meaning of RAUMLICHKEIT. For all his antipathy to the Newtonian conception of nature, Heidegger constantly stresses the essential spatiality or spatialness (*Räumlichkeit*) of human existence. We should note, however, that it is precisely the non-Newtonian aspects of spatialness that define the field of human operations as Heidegger and Boss see it. Man for Heidegger is defined as spatial but not confined in space. As a physical object, to be sure, man is extended, locatable, changing position relative to other physical objects, and the like, but none of these characteristics is distinctive of his humanness or descriptive of the way in which he actually operates. *Qua* human, human spatialness refers to human existence as clarifying, understanding, and open to meaningful (and possibly fulfilling) relations with concrete entities encountered in space. But human perception, understanding, intention, appreciation, even pragmatic utilization are across space, not in it, transcendent of it while cognizant of it and able to deal with it. In English, "spatialness," though not commonly used, has a slightly less abstract or geometrical sound than "spatiality" and might better convey the human quality of Heidegger's *Räumlichkeit.*

The meaning of LEIBLICHKEIT. Closely akin to spatialness, *Leiblichkeit* ("bodiliness" or "bodyhood") has in the Boss-Heidegger scheme very little to do with the conception of the body as a physical object contained by the skin, occupying and moving through space. Human being present (*Dasein*) is being open to things, including oneself, both cognitively and motivationally. But the things we deal with generally are physical entities or qualities, like other people and the characteristics of concrete entities (*Seiendes*) that we perceive through our senses. Even when we go beyond perception to recall things that are not present, what we re-experience representatively always involves the physical qualities or character of things. Going further than this, when we deal with mathematical abstractions or purely ideal relationships like "truth" and "beauty," our conceptions are related to perceptual experiences, to spoken or written language, and similar events or situations that are essentially physical.[19] It follows that our distinctively human presence (to the self as well as to the other) is basically physical or bodily, though by no means limited to the physical boundaries of our own body. On the contrary, our bodily colored or toned awareness and concern are constantly reaching out toward entities and situations beyond the limits of our own skin. As Boss has indicated, to sit down with a loved one to plan a long-desired vacation is certainly to be in physical proximity to another body and to be concerned with matters that are essentially physical: travel, living arrangements, length of stay, recreational activities, and the like; but it is also to quite transcend the physical limitations of the two bodies most involved and the corner of the living room in which they are temporarily located. So human physicalness—and this seems to be a better translation of *Leiblichkeit* than "bodiliness" or "bodyhood"—is not something that is contained in a restricted area but that reaches out toward the distant and the different through its perceptions and understanding, its desires and intentions. Boss calls this not a restriction but a "bodying forth" (*Leiben*) of our humanness. Like temporality, physicalness is not a thing but a *way in which we are* as physical

19. This does not mean entirely or exclusively physical but having a physical aspect or manifestation. Words are both physical and carriers of impalpable meaning.

beings who are also capable of understanding and self-fulfillment. The staples of physical science, space, time, and matter, are thus given a radically different significance from the Newtonian in Heidegger's treatment of spatialness, temporality, and physicalness.

The meaning of VERGEGENWAERTIGEN *and* DAS GEDAECHTNIS. To Boss and Heidegger all representation involves retention in human awareness of things experienced; that is to say, representation implies *object retention*. By contrast, most psychologically oriented thinkers since the time of Locke have been preoccupied with the mental representations themselves (ideas, images, *Vorstellungen*) rather than with the objects to which they refer. Consequently, they have construed remembering, thinking, reasoning, and many other mental acts as the revival, association, and interaction of these intramental "ideas." Heidegger and Boss insist, on the other hand, that because the human existent is primarily a kind of openness to the understanding of things encountered in the world, thinking is not picturing things but understanding their meaning, which means letting things come into the openness of human existence as they are.[20] What has been once experienced, however, continues to be present in some way. When what has been present for some time is merely background it is, in Heidegger's terminology, *unthematic* (*unthematisch*), but when it is again focused upon clearly and explicitly, it becomes *thematic,* and we are again "there" (*da*) "with" (*bei*) this thing, allowing it to occupy our attention in a manner comparable to what took place when it was first experienced. This is "re-presenting" the experienced object to ourselves. This is not memory, however, but simply representation. Speaking fairly strictly, memory would seem to be that special form of representation in which the experienced situation or object is recognized as having occurred at a specific time in the past. Here Heidegger and Boss are close to the Aristotelian notion of memory as different from reproductive imagination or simple representation in that recognition of the past *as such* is always involved in memory, but not in the ordinary revival of objects previously experienced, which is simply representation.

20. Martin Heidegger, *Was heisst Denken?* (Tübingen: Niemeyer, 1954).

Boss further indicates that we often speak loosely when we say that someone has *forgotten* something, such as, an umbrella, since we do not mean that the person has no memory, or is unable to form a representation of this object. We indicate rather that at a given time other things are pre-empting his or her attention, so that retention of this object is not thematic, that is, not clear and central. When I am unable to bring an experienced object once more to clear awareness, it is the retention that is defective since certain aspects of the revived experience remain vague or unthematic. Retention, then, is the basis of both representation and memory. But representation is not picturing but re-living an experience, while memory is re-living an experience while recognizing its past context, which I think can be well described in English as *recollection*. I therefore translate Heidegger's *vergegenwärtigen* by *to revive* or *to re-live* (an experience), and *das Gedächtnis* by *recollection*.

Finally, the retention of experience through both revival and recollection is the expression of the essentially historical nature or *historicity* (*Geschichtlichkeit*) of human existence, since through retention man—individual and group—carries with him his past experience or history.

The meaning of DIE FREIHEIT. Both Heidegger and Boss seem more concerned with the ontological foundations of freedom (*die Freiheit*) than with free choice or free will (*der freie Wille*) in the usual sense. The capacity of the human self-reflective presence to allow other things to be just as they are in coming within its realm of openness is not only illustrative of freedom in their first sense (*die Freiheit*), which is freedom *for* or freedom *to,* but is the indispensable condition for the *possibility* of freedom in the sense of free will. It is *die Angst* (dismayed apprehensiveness), says Heidegger (*SuZ,* 188), that reveals in *Dasein* its Being towards its ownmost possibility of Being, which means its being free (*Freisein*) for the freedom (*Freiheit*) of choosing and grasping itself and for the authenticity (*Eigentlichkeit*) of its Being as possibility (*Möglichkeit*). As we saw in our earlier discussion of *Angst,* this also is freedom *to.*

What, then, of freedom *from* constraint or coercion, external or internal? *Sein und Zeit* has little to say about free will, while Boss seems content to note that free choice in the usual or factual (*faktisch*) sense of the term is a matter of everyday experience. This is a less than satisfactory answer, since determinists generally do not deny that human beings experience apparent freedom (of choice or will), but argue that the experience is implicatively deceptive, i.e., deceptive not as an experience but in what it implies, namely, that I really have free choice. Analogously, a feeling of unlimited power or competence, however real it might be, does not carry any assurance of actual power or competence. How could I prove that I can easily learn to play the oboe or write a successful novel? Certainly not just by the clarity or intensity or the feeling involved. Does it not therefore require more than the feeling that I can do what I want to do—rather than what I have been conditioned to do by training, habit, threat, or whatever—to prove that I am free? Boss seems to be well acquainted with this line of reasoning, so that his keeping the argument on a common-sense level may only be reflecting Heidegger's own scepticism about the demonstrability of free choice or free will. It is possible, then, that Heidegger failed to develop a set of "ontic" arguments for actual freedom because when he reviewed the actual and possible arguments for it he found them wanting. If it is true that neither determinism nor free will is truly provable, Boss is perhaps adopting the conservative position that at least the experience of apparent freedom has to be admitted and dealt with, and he does not seem to deny that it may be dealt with far more extensively than he has chosen to do.

The meaning of ONTOLOGISCH, ONTISCH, EXISTENZIAL, *and* EXISTENZ-IELL. Corresponding to the distinction between *Sein* ("Being") and *Seiendes* ("entity") in Heidegger's thought is that between *ontologisch* ("ontological") and *ontisch* ("ontic"). Looking at reality from the standpoint of the Being (*Sein*) which underlies all things is the *ontological* perspective, while looking at reality from the standpoint of the entities (*Seiendes*) we actually experience all around us is the *ontic* perspective (*SuZ*, 11). Belonging to the ontological perspective is the adjective *existenzial* (existential); to the ontic perspective, *existenziell* (*SuZ*, 13). The suffix *-ell* is fairly common in German for the formation of an adjective from a non-German (usually Latin) noun. Thus *Form* yields the adjective *formell,* and similar derivatives are *sexuell, potentiell,* and *experimentell.* But there is no corresponding form in English; hence the translation of *existenziell* (German) by "existentiell" (English) is linguistically nonsensical.

However, the English suffix -ate, ordinarily indicating a verb (cele-brate, hesitate, donate), may be used as an adjectival ending (pin-nate, sensate, obdurate, cingulate) whether there is another adjec-tive with the same stem (sensual-sensate, social-sociate) or not (irate, desperate). Besides "existential," therefore, we could create an adjective from *existence,* "existentiate," and use that to translate the German *existenziell.* We would then have the double pairs:

> *ontologisch* (ontological)   *existenzial* (existential)
> *ontisch* (ontic)   *existenziell* (existentiate)[21]

Glossary of
Basic Heidegerrian Terminology

I have dealt at varying length with some fifty to sixty terms from Heidegger's *Sein und Zeit* which I regard as most pertinent to the psychological dimension of his thought and easily mistranslated or misunderstood. In alphabetical order, with a few opposites and adjectival or nominal equivalents omitted, these are:

ableben	giving up life
Angst	dismayed apprehensiveness
Befindlichkeit	sense of one's situation
Besorgen	taking care of things
Dasein	human presence or being present
Durchsichtigkeit	self-transparency
Entschlossenheit	deliberate self-affirmation

---

21. It is curious that the neologism in German is *existenzial,* which Heidegger coined (apparently after the English model) to describe that which pertains *ontolog-ically (ontologisch)* to human existence. Heidegger then used the regular form *exis-tenziell* to denote that which pertains to the human being contingently, as a matter of ordinary experience, and not on the basis of ontological necessity. By contrast, our coined word "existentiate" is to translate *existenziell* (which ordinarily would be translated by the English "existential," which latter cannot be used for this pur-pose since it has been pre-empted to translate Heidegger's neologism *existenzial*). This is clearly a sufficient muddle which is not helped by creating a class of adjec-tives in English ending in *ell,* a class having an *n* of 1.

entwerfen	to project oneself
Erschlossenheit	deliberate self-disclosure
Existenz	self-anticipatory human existence
Existenzial	a prerequisite of human existence
existenzial	pertaining to the very Being of man
existenziell	pertaining to human existence as ordinarily experienced.
Faktizität	"facticity," the state of having actually occurred
Freiheit	freedom to
freier Wille	freedom from
Fürsorge	concern for others
Gedächtnis	recollection
Gestimmtheit	disposition
Gewissen	the thrust toward self-realization
Gewissensruf	the call to self-realization
Geworfenheit	condition or situation as predetermined
Leiblichkeit	human physicalness
Lichtung	openness to meaning
das Man	the impersonal Other, the They (as in "*They* say you should never argue religion or politics")
Mitdasein	person other than I
Miteinandersein	being together with others
Mitsein	the general state of human togetherness
Mitwelt	the human environment
Nachsicht	looking after others
Nichtigkeit	nothingness
Nichts	nothing
ontisch	pertaining to beings (entities) as experienced

ontologisch	pertaining to the nature of Being
Räumlichkeit	spatialness
Rücksicht	considerateness
Schuld	responsibility for self-realization
Seiende(s)	entity
Sein	Being
Sorge	involved commitment
sterben	human dying
Stimmung	emotional disposition
thematisch	clearly focused
Tod(e)	human death
Umsicht	looking over a situation with circumspection
Umwelt	the nonhuman environment
Unheimlichkeit	the weirdness of the unfamiliar
verenden	the dying unaware of the nonhuman
Verfallenheit	victimization, forfeiture
vergegenwärtigen	to relive an experience
Verstehen	appreciation of the possible
vorhanden	merely present
Welt	field or context of human activity
Zeitlichkeit	human temporality
zuhanden	humanly useful, practicable

3

Existential Phenomenology and the Conceptual Foundations of Psychology

Phenomenological Psychology as a Preparatory (Propaedeutic) Discipline

We began our primer of existential phenomenology for psychologists with a "hitting the high points" review of modern theories of human psychological functioning. The purpose was to provide a background (or "horizon") for understanding the Heideggerian approach to man and to make clear the continuing existence of a non-physicalistic, non-mechanistic, non-reductionistic tradition in psychology. Our next problem was to find common American-English equivalents for the basic terms of Heidegger's system, many of which were cast by him in a striking but idiosyncratic German. Our final and most difficult task is to say something meaningful about the possible impact of the Heidegger-Boss approach on the conceptual foundations of a contemporary psychology. I say "possible" because so far the influence of this unique and highly integrated theory on psychology in this country has been slight indeed. True, there has been interest in (and admiration for) the work of Binswanger and Boss in some clinical circles, but their effect on the psychological establishment, academic and professional, has been remarkably lacking in specificity and conceptual focus, providing chiefly a kind of philosophico-literary titillation for the humanistically inclined among us. Even for those who are most convinced of the validity of the phenomenological approach, an existential-phenomenological *psychology* stands for a program to be developed, a set of recommendations to be followed. Phenomenological psychology would at this point seem to be a propaedeutic or prelude to empirical psychology, a pre-science or *Vorwissenschaft,* that could provide the impetus and the rationale for a "new and improved" scientific psychology. This new psychology would result from the application of the scientific (i.e., empirical) method to psychological phenomena as such, which is to say as they are in themselves and not as construed according to a model or paradigm derived from other sciences such as physics or biology. In initial support of the program and recommendations for a phenomenological psychology I can only point to inadequacies and fallacies in various current theories and methods in psychology that violate phenomenological principles, and suggest in general fashion ways in which the hermeneutic or phenomenological method might preclude or escape such logical and factual embarrassments.

Paradigmatics, Hermeneutics, and the Hypotheticodeductive Method

Orignally the term "paradigm" meant simply a pattern, model, or example. Its classical application was to the grammatical models of declension and conjugation that were important in the study of Greek and Latin, and as late as the turn of the century this was the only meaning given to the term. In recent years, however, the notion of paradigm has been extended, one might almost say "exalted," into a general and indispensable component of scientific procedure. It is the key concept in Thomas Kuhn's very influential *The Structure of Scientific Revolutions* (1970),[1] and it has come to be the object of an obsessively abiding interest for psychologists. Though Kuhn's book is concerned almost exclusively with the physical sciences, it has seemed to many psychologists that the concept of paradigm, which for Kuhn plays so important a role in these sciences, has abundant analogues in psychology, such as the

1. Thomas S. Kuhn, *The Structure of Scientific Revolutions,* 2nd ed. (Chicago: University of Chicago Press, 1970).

operant conditioning model, the social learning model, the psycho-analytic model, and many others; some even argue that this *embarras de richesses* of paradigmatic theories in psychology may be less embarrassing and more enriching than hitherto suspected, that the very plethora of psychological paradigms may make psychology comparable to the more mature sciences, a status that psychologists have been pining for at least since the days of Johann Friedrich Herbart.

There can be little doubt that the looseness of Kuhn's conception of "paradigm," as betrayed by the variability of his examples, has encouraged those who seek to assimilate their own versions of paradigm to Kuhn's "scientific" archetype. Regarding the ambiguity of Kuhn's message, one critic has claimed that Kuhn uses the term "paradigm" in at least twenty-one different senses.[2] From the standpoint of denotation or extension, this allegation may be supportable. Kuhn unquestionably laid himself open to this criticism by failing to offer anywhere a plain definition of "paradigm."

One's first impression is that Kuhn's "paradigm" is a philosophical notion, but he hastens to assure the reader that a specifically scientific set of convictions must be held by a considerable segment of the scientific community before that community can undertake the primary task of what Kuhn calls *normal science,* i.e., the production of research. "Normal science," he says, "means research firmly based upon one or more past scientific achievements." The foundational beliefs required, he adds, "expound the body of accepted theory, illustrate many or all of its successful applications, and compare these applications with exemplary observations and experiments." The recommended body of theory and research methods would be found today in science textbooks; in earlier times it would have been set forth in famous classics of science such as Aristotle's *Physica,* Ptolemy's *Almagest,* Newton's *Principia,* or Lavoisier's *Traité de chimie.*[3] In any case, the theories

2. Margaret Masterman, "The Nature of a Paradigm," in *Criticism and the Growth of Knowledge,* ed. I. Lakatos and A. Musgrave (Cambridge: The University Press, 1970), pp. 59–89.

3. Aristotle, *The Physics,* trans. P. H. Wicksteed and F. M. Cornford (Cambridge, Mass.: Harvard University Press, 1934); Ptolemy (Claudius Ptolemaeus),

and methods referred to are not metaphysical or epistemological in nature, but derive from "accepted examples of actual scientific practice," and "provide models from which spring particular coherent traditions of scientific research," like Copernican astronomy or Newtonian dynamics.

Rather than directly defining "paradigm," Kuhn provides us with two external criteria for identifying paradigms by noting, first, that the achievements of "normal science" must be "sufficiently unprecedented to attract an enduring group of adherents," and, second, "sufficiently open-ended to leave all sorts of problems . . . to resolve." He then summarizes: "Achievements that have these two characteristics I shall henceforth refer to as 'paradigms.' " This, surely, is a curious substitute for a definition, one which characterizes paradigms by what we might call their "social stimulus value" in attracting "an enduring group of adherents" and their fortunate deficiency of leaving "all sorts of problems" unresolved and therefore open to be resolved.

We are left in the dark as to how general a paradigm must be in order to achieve paradigmatic status. Even when Kuhn is talking about paradigms with high scientific content and research reference, he applies the term to very general statements of theoretical and methodological (but still empirical) principle, such as those set forth in Newton's *Principia,* and also to quite particular distinctions like that between Priestley's "dephlogisticated air" and Lavoisier's "acid-forming air" or "oxygen."[4]

If we consider only those paradigms of a general or comprehensive nature, having immediate reference to the empirical sciences and their historical development, particularly since the sixteenth century, it becomes clear that in these contexts Kuhn's paradigm is not adequately differentiated from the notion of "partly validated hypothesis." Moreover, such a hypothesis must be regarded as an integral aspect of the classical *hypotheticodeductive method,* the methodological procedure at the heart of the great advances of the

The Almagest, trans. R. C. Taliafero (Chicago: Encyclopaedia Britannica Inc., 1952); Newton, *Philosophiae Naturalis Principia;* Antoine L. Lavoisier, *Traité elementaire de chimie* (1789), trans. R. Kerr, *Elements of Chemistry* (New York: Dover Publications, 1965).

4. Kuhn, *Structure,* pp. 10 ff.

natural sciences since the time of Copernicus. In the hypotheti-codeductive method the hypothesis is simply the general theoret-ical statement from which consequences can be deduced whose validity can be tested in experience; thus Kuhn's *paradigm* is in great part coextensive with the *hypothesis* intrinsic to the hypotheti-codeductive method. To employ that method is to deduce from the paradigm or hypothesis certain consequences of an empirically measurable or denotable nature. Empirical phenomena are then investigated inductively in order to determine whether (and to what extent) the deductively inferred consequences are (induc-tively) verifiable. Like all inductions (other than the complete in-duction of mathematics), this last procedure is a probablistic and approximate one. Of course, we never verify a hypothesis or par-adigm but only certain consequences deduced from it which may be said to support (without fully validating) the hypothesis or par-adigm itself.

In order to employ the hypotheticodeductive method the scien-tific investigator must, before formulating a meaningful hypoth-esis, acquire a considerable amount of inductively derived infor-mation regarding the field that the hypothesis applies to, as well as acquaintance with various methodological techniques used in the empirical investigation of natural phenomena. It is obviously for this reason that (for example) a person without extensive knowl-edge of the general chemical properties of objects could not formu-late a sensible hypothesis or paradigm explaining chemical re-actions or devise a practicable way of testing any such hypothesis.

We note that though the hypothesis is developed deductively, it has its roots in inductive information and its verification in induc-tive testing. There is reason, however, for stressing deduction, since the explanation for which science strives is always deductive. Induction can tell us what is so; it cannot tell us why. When, how-ever, we deduce why (reasoning from the general to the particu-lar), we must then examine the particulars inductively to see whether what we predicted is actually so.

The formation of a scientific hypothesis that can be tested em-pirically is by no stretch of the imagination a regular result of fac-tual (inductive) and technical (methodological) information. Fruit-ful hypotheses are nearly always dependent for their origin on creative intuition, which bridges the gap between the factual and the explanatory by an anticipatory insight of the *aha!* type. Thus many methodologically informed and astute physicists at the turn of the century were fully acquainted with difficulties in Newtonian theory regarding such matters as the nature of space, the concept of absolute rest, and the relation between the speed of light and other very rapid motions; but it took the creative insight and mathematical brilliance of Einstein to take these and many other considerations into account: to reformulate the concept of space, to reject the notions of absolute rest and simultaneity, and to view the speed of light as radically different from any other motion in the universe; and then, having intuitively divined the outlines of this new and revolutionary image of physical reality, to formulate the hypothesis of special relativity in precise scientific (in this case, mathematical) language, using the methods of non-Euclidean geometry, borrowed from Riemann, and the tensor calculus, picked up as it were incidentally from an obscure Swiss mathematician while Einstein was a student in Zurich. Many years later Einstein would confide to Max Wertheimer that between his intuitive projection of the new world view and the formulation of the theory (or hypothesis or paradigm) of special relativity, there were eight steps of pure mathematical deduction to be gone through, a sequence which no one before him had ever put together, and all this before Einstein could offer a single empirically testable or measurable prediction.[5]

Regarding Kuhn's "scientific revolutions," it would seem that his conception of the role of the paradigm in them amounts to a loosely stated and somewhat truncated version of the hypothetico-deductive method, viewed in historical perspective and with particular application to systematic hypotheses in the physical sciences. And what shall we say of the relevance of the concept of paradigm for psychology? If, as I have argued, the notion of paradigm is integral to the hypotheticodeductive method, it is clear that many psychologists have looked upon that method not only as appropriate to psychology but as a chief means of developing the full potential of psychology as a behavior science. Thus in the

5. Max Wertheimer. *Productive Thinking* (New York: Harper and Row, 1945).

1950s psychologists like Melvin Marx and Hall and Lindzey attempted to redefine the procedures of psychological science in accordance with the requirements of the hypotheticodeductive method as they understood it, this understanding being conditioned by a remarkably recent acquaintance with logical positivism and a boundless admiration for the concept of "operational definition," as defined (nonoperationally) by Percy Bridgman in his *Logic of Modern Physics* (1927).[6] It is indeed ironic that logical positivism and operationism were repudiated by their creators, notably Herbert Feigl and Rudolph Carnap, members of the original Vienna Circle, and Percy Bridgman, the supreme operationist, just about the time that others were taking up those ideas and elevating them into regnant principles.[7] Not only minor lights like Marx and Lindzey but the great Clark Hull, whom many regard as psychology's most creative systematist, believed firmly in the value of the hypotheticodeductive method for the conceptual understanding of experimental investigation and theorizing in psychology. Hull's faith extended to the affirmation that the principles governing all learning (in the human as well as in the albino rat) could be demonstrated scientifically by hypotheticodeductive procedures. This indeed was the primary message of his *Principles of Behavior.*[8]

We are, however, in for a rude awakening when we begin to apply the notions of paradigm and the hypotheticodeductive method, as exemplified by the great theorists in the natural sciences, to Hull's "principles" and theories. Even if we assume that Hull's *constructs* (a more accurate name in this case than "principles" or "theories") have a greater validity and a wider applicability than has so far been proven, the almost total absence of explanatory force, the extremely limited generality, and the logical obscurity of key concepts such as "habit strength" and "reactive inhibition" render Hull's system a trivial parody of what can

6. Melvin Marx, ed., *Psychological Theory* (New York: Macmillan, 1950); Calvin S. Hall and Gardner Lindzey, *Theories of Personality* (New York: Wiley, 1957); Percy Bridgman, *The Logic of Modern Physics* (New York: Macmillan, 1927).

7. Sigmund Koch, in *Behaviorism and Phenomenology,* ed. Wann, pp. 47–74.

8. Clark L. Hull. *Principles of Behavior* (New York: Appleton-Century-Crofts, 1943).

be accomplished with the hypotheticodeductive method in the physical sciences.

Without attempting to document the history of the hypothetico-deductive method, let me briefly attempt a kind of pre-Kuhnian but broadly hermeneutic analysis of the way in which the hypotheticodeductive method may serve as a vehicle for the emergence of a new major theory in physical science. I am sure that this analysis owes a great deal to Max Wertheimer's *Productive Thinking,* to Sir Arthur Eddington's *The Nature of the Physical World,*[9] and to Sir James Jeans's *The Mysterious Universe,*[10] but I have borrwed from these and other sources in the logic of scientific method in a fashion that I can no longer clearly remember. These authors therefore bear no responsibility for the particularities of the views set forth. My hope is that the analysis will help to clarify the extent to which behavior sciences such as psychology may aspire to effective use of the hypotheticodeductive method. Let me begin by distinguishing five stages in the emergence of a hypotheticodeductively determined scientific theory:

Stage 1. The inductive phase. Here the general descriptive properties of the field are mastered. Here also are found the inductive anomalies respecting older theory or theories, i.e., the failure of accepted theory (hypothesis or paradigm) correctly to predict empirical data. As a result, the consequences deduced from the old hypothesis are not verified by inductive examination.

Stage 2. The intuitive phase. Here the scientist, having reviewed the data, retested the methods of analysis and the techniques of empirical manipulation, and reexamined all the anomalies to which the accepted hypothesis seems to lead, has a sudden intuition of a radically different view from the accepted one, a creative insight into what may be a solution to all the problems the older theory raises without answering.

Stage 3. The formalization phase. Here we move from "rough and ready" statement to more precise and technical formulation. The hypothesis is framed in quantitatively exact and/or logically quali-

9. Arthur S. Eddington, *The Nature of the Physical World* (New York: Macmillan, 1928).

10. James Jeans, *The Mysterious Universe* (New York: Macmillan, 1930).

fied language; its distinctness from the accepted view is explained, and its consonance with known data and principles clarified. The precise import of the hypothesis, conceptually speaking at least, is now known.

Stage 4. The deductive phase. This stage is continuous with the formalization stage, but moves dynamically from the formal toward the empirical. The hypothesis is analyzed mathematically, where this is possible, but in any case, deductively, and the ultimate term of the deduction is a set of consequences that can be empirically assayed The logical form is:

$$\text{If H, then } C_1, C_2, C_3, \ldots C_N$$
$$\text{But } C_1, C_2, C_3 \ldots C_N$$
$$\therefore \text{ H}$$

That is, if we assume our hypothesis (H) to be true, then certain empirically determinable consequences (C_1, C_2, etc.) follow from it; but these predicted consequences are found upon examination to hold. Therefore, the hypothesis is itself upheld. It should be evident that the logical form is not apodictic or strictly demonstrative. The hypothesis is not proved or verified, but it approaches verification as the number of deduced consequences, found to hold in experience, increases. Though the empirical consequences are originally deduced, the reasoning is ultimately inductive because dependent on the enumeration of particulars, an enumeration that can never be exhaustive.

Stage 5. The empirical testing phase. This is highlighted by the sometimes enormously complicated task of examining the relevant area of experience by controlled (and where possible, quantitative) methods in order to determine whether—and with what degree of exactitude—the empirical data agree with the predictions derived by deduction from the hypothesis. In the case of Einstein's special theory of relativity, for example, several of the key predictions made in 1905 were not actually tested until 1919, at which time their much greater agreement with astronomical data than that of predictions derived from Newtonian theory revealed to the world that a new view of the physical universe was to supersede Newton's vision, which had held undisputed sway in physical science for more than two hundred years.

If we now attempt to identify what in psychology corresponds to these five stages of the hypotheticodeductive method, we are soon struck by the realization that as far as contemporary psychology is concerned we must dispense with four of the five stages, and indeed we can progress only a short distance into the first stage before finding that *there are simply no examples in psychology of genuinely universal laws.* Intuition of a sort is, to be sure, within the compass of today's psychologist—some would say that intuitive surmise is as close as psychology ever gets to understanding the reason for anything!—but the psychologist's intuitions are not grounded in inductively established generalizations, nor can he formalize psychological intuition into hypothetical statements of principle from which empirically testable consequences can be deduced or predicted.

What then *is* the hypotheticodeductive method in psychology? There is no escaping the conclusion that it has so far amounted to no more than a preliminary subphase of the first or inductive stage of that method. Since psychology has never achieved an unexceptionable generalization even of the descriptive sort, it has no universal propositions from which it can proceed toward the particular. I am not referring merely to the absence of commanding generalizations like Boyle's law in physics, the "all or none" law in neurology, or the law regarding the helical structure of DNA in biochemistry, but to simple inductive descriptions like those setting forth the electrical conductance of metals, the live-bearing properties of mammals (exception being made of monotremes like the platypus), or the morphological characteristics of the many thousands of species of insects. The inductively derived laws of the physical and biological sciences certainly apply to man as a physiologically functioning body, but there are no comparable psychological laws, no general statements (not already known to common sense) that psychology can advance regarding human intelligence, motivation, emotion, or attitude. Thus psychometric generalizations, which are among psychology's most well validated consensually, hold for the group without holding for all the individuals in the group, a kind of logical collectiveness (as opposed to divisiveness) which makes them slippery footing indeed for deductive analysis. Consider "The college graduate has a higher IQ than the person who never got beyond the sixth grade" versus "Tungsten has a higher electrical resistance than copper." Nor can the generalizations of abnormal psychology or the experimental psychology of learning be considered to be free of this logical infirmity. The complexly multivariate nature of the subject-matter and the crudity of the classification system employed in psychopathology make an irreducible difference between "Manic patients are extremely active" and "Fluorine is an extremely active halogen" or between "The first units in a list of nonsense syllables are learned faster than units toward the middle of the list" and "The first stages of radioactive decay are the alpha particle stages." Philosophical psychology can rightly argue that empirical psychology achieves no more than the tendential or quasi universality of group generalizations which hold only in the round, while the physical, and even the biological, sciences are able to describe properties and relations in a fashion which, if not absolutely unexceptionable, approaches far more closely than psychology the asymptote of authentic generalization. The scientifically oriented psychologist may woo the universal ardently, but the courtship remains without embrace.

The alleged conformity of psychometric predictions to the hypotheticodeductive method of proceeding from the universal to the particular will not sustain critical scrutiny. Correctly stated, psychometric prediction proceeds from the *pseudo*-universal of the collectivity to some (but not all) individuals in the group; and this is hypotheticodeductive metaphor rather than method. Psychometric "universals" are quantitative descriptions of group tendencies which may hold for a sizable number of individuals in one group as they did for a somewhat similar group, but they will not hold for all the individuals in either group and we cannot say for which individuals in particular they will hold. To say that Tomkins (whose score on a college aptitude test places him in the upper 10 percent of the standardization group) will do better in college than Peterson (whose score on the same test is in the lowest quarter of the group) is the kind of prediction that few of us would stake our chances of salvation on, despite the assurance of the psychometricians that the "confidence level" is 95 percent or higher. Even when we make only cautious predictions, based on very careful measurements, we are not deducing in any strict sense but extrapolating from one set of circumstances to another that partially resembles the first, a procedure that, whatever its pragmatic value, is devoid of theoretical content, since the warrant for the prediction is that similar prognostications have been wrong only five times in a hundred!

No doubt there is in many sciences—especially in their practical or technological aspects—a certain amount of what I may call "inadequate induction" (or sampling) which could not possibly justify authentic generalization but which might plausibly suggest extrapolation to similar situations not yet observed. These extrapolations may also be later supported or "verified" within very loosely specified limits of confidence. If this, however, is the closest the science can come to deductive prediction and inductive verification, we have little more than a caricature of the hypothetico-deductive method, bearing only the faintest resemblance to the mathematical elegance of nuclear physics or the experimental precision of physical chemistry or even microbiology.

All this is certainly no reason to discount the importance of induction, which plays a vital and continuing role in all sciences, first, in the pre-theoretical ordering and cataloguing of empirical data, and second, in the verification of theoretically deduced consequences. There is, nonetheless, a universe of difference between employing an induction, which involves a sufficient enumeration of particulars, in order to verify a connection deduced from theory (as in the physical sciences), and the use of a deductive (only because mathematical) extrapolation, *sans* theory, to fill the gaps in an insufficiently enumerated induction or sampling. In the latter case, the deduction involved is not only pre-theoretical, it is also pre-inductive, and, to the extent that we regard science as a system of generalizations of an at least potentially explanatory nature, pre-scientific. Methodologically speaking, the best psychology may be regarded as teleologically scientific or scientific-in-intention, but for a science *in fieri* to "affect the nod" regarding its mathematicodeductive theories, the latter taken in a sense univocal with that of the developed sciences, smacks of juvenile fantasy identification.[11]

11. Raymond J. McCall, "The Nature of Psychology: A Sceptical Clinician's View," *Journal of Clinical Psychology* 20 (1964): 311–25.

What now of this other widespread use of "paradigm" in psychology, to describe theories alleged to be scientifically relevant or becoming scientific, if not actually scientific? Most behaviorists, we know, consider themselves as experimental scientists and think of their behaviorism as an extension of their commitment to scientific psychology. Can we say then that behaviorism provides a paradigm whose implications can be tested in many diverse areas of psychology, from the experimental investigation of conditioning, through the technological aspects of programmed instruction, into psychotherapy and the management of the retarded and the emotionally disturbed? Such global questions invite a too ready assent to behaviorists' claims of functioning in a properly scientific fashion. In the first place, the connection between behaviorist theory and any specific scientific investigation is a heuristic rather than a logical dependence, designed to persuade and to illustrate rather than to demonstrate, strictly speaking. There is also a great difference between using behavioral methods and being committed to behaviorism. It is true that behavior in the sense of externally observable activity does lend itself more readily to scientific observation than do data derived from introspection or the analysis of consciousness, and behaviorist thinkers like Watson, Hull, and Skinner have powerfully influenced experimental methods in psychology. Having conceded that much, I must insist that there is an enormous difference between behavioral methods, which many psychologists of a wide variety of theoretical and philosophical persuasions can employ effectively, and the dogmatic pontifications of philosophical behaviorism as set forth in Watson's *Behaviorism* or Skinner's *Beyond Freedom and Dignity*.[12] Behavioral methods are accepted, up to a point at least, by virtually everybody and are clearly here to stay. The real question remaining is that of the impact of behaviorist *ontology* and *philosophical methodology* on contemporary psychology. Here behaviorism becomes the paragon of the non-hermeneutic or anti-phenomenological approach to the study of human activity, an approach which recasts experience in the light of its mechanistic and reductionistic

---

12. John B. Watson, *Behaviorism* (New York: Norton, 1924); Burrhus F. Skinner, Beyond Freedom and Dignity (New York: Knopf, 1971).

model (or paradigm) of human function. In what follows I will try to gauge the influence of this model on the experimental investigation of learning, and I will argue that this influence has been as pernicious as it has been enormous.

Psychoanalytic Physicalism

Though very different from behaviorism in inspiration and interest, psychoanalysis has an equally ontological bent and again, like behaviorism, favors a mechanistic and reductionistic model or paradigm in its approach to the understanding of that which is most fundamental to and definitive of the human being. Though lacking in experimental psychological foundations or applications, psychoanalysts consider their discipline scientific in origin and are absolutely confident that its insights and explanations will eventually be supported by scientific developments. Like behaviorists, too, psychoanalysts have been tireless in applying their "principles" to every aspect of the human condition, not only to psychopathology and psychotherapy, but to normal personality development, and to history, anthropology, religion, literature, and the arts. Psychoanalysis has also been immensely influential in psychology, most especially in clinical psychology and the psychology of personality, though its originally stimulating effect on these latter two areas has become stultifying.

Freud believed that the psychologically most important fact about human beings is their motivation, a consideration that the new scientific psychology of his day had completely ignored. Freud's important belief that many of our motives are unconscious was acquired from Bernheim and Liébeault in the 1880s. Far more important than the idea of unconscious motivation were Freud's hypothesis that these unconscous motives were symbolized in the individual's fantasies and behavior and his confidence that the psychoanalytic method provided a key for deciphering these symbolic meanings. It is thus that Freud's first two books, *The Interpretation of Dreams* and *The Psychopathology of Everyday Life,* are concerned with the analytic process of interpretation or desymbolization, first of dreams, and second of everyday parapraxes or "failed acts," like slips of the tongue and memory lapses. Trained as a deterministic scientist, Freud believed that human action, however irrational it might seem, was never without reason, and was therefore lawful and within the possible compass of scientific understanding. Freud had also been led to believe that the most elementary principle governing human motivation is the *pleasure principle,* that we act to maximize pleasure and minimize pain. Like most hedonists, however, Freud added that awareness of reality makes us recognize that sometimes pleasure-seeking action has to be inhibited until the conditions for pleasure (or motive satisfaction) are at hand. Thus human motivation is regulated by a *reality principle,* whereby gratification is postponed until the situation is ripe, as truly as it involves and is based on a pleasure principle.

Freud had been thoroughly trained not just in science but in the physicalism of Ernst Brücke, Helmholtz's friend and disciple, who held that scientific explanation must always rest on physical laws and that nothing could be postulated as operative in the organism beyond the ordinary physicochemical properties of matter. It is therefore not surprising that Freud sought a neurological equivalent of the pleasure principle and the reality principle, a neurological equivalent that would be construed according to the laws of physical energy exchange, as set forth by Brücke and Helmholtz. The specification of this neurological system was outlined by Freud in his *Entwurf einer Psychologie* (*Project for a Scientific Psychology,* 1895). The disposition of neurons to discharge energy as soon as it reached a critical level was seen as the neural foundation of the *Lustprinzip,* while the capacity of contact barriers (later called "synapses") to inhibit the discharge of energy constituted a partial basis for the reality principle or the postponement of action. Freud never published his *Entwurf* and he later repudiated the specific identification of neuronal structures with the functional units of his motivational system, but he never forsook the idea of energy balance and exchange (which, strangely, he called "economics") as the key to human motivation, psychopathological and normal. Energy was for him the basis of pain (energy increases) and pleasure (energy release), of fixation and regression, displacement, conversion, cathexis and countercathexis, sublimation and abreaction, inhibition and expression. Also, the key concept of *libido* was iden-

tified with the psychic energy of the sex drive and, though removed from identifiable and measurable physical force, it was
clearly a psychic *Doppelgänger* of Helmholtz's *Kraft,* an energy that
could be conserved (in accordance with the supreme principle of
Helmholtzian physics, the conservation of energy), stored up,
drained off, diverted, held back, counterbalanced, parceled out, or
returned to its source. In its operations, in short, Freud's "psychic
energy" is about as non-physical as water pressure or electric current. The German *Kraft* is close to being synonymous with the
Greek *dynamis,* so that Freudian *psychodynamics* (or motivational
theory) is in the last analysis not very different from "psychohy-
draulics." We should not therefore be misled by Freud's ostensible
renunciation of the notion of "psychical processes as quantitatively determined states of specifiable material particles . . ."[13]
into thinking that he ever construed the "psychic apparatus" as
anything but a physical system; even in the 1930s Freud was still
referring to pleasure as energy discharge, pain as energy buildup,
cathexis as energy investment, and every significant human action
as a species of energy exchange. What we have then in the psychoanalytic theory of human motivation is an energic or hydraulic
model, a metaphorical extrapolation from Brückean physicalistic
physiology, a paradigm imposed on the data of human action and
interaction without a shred of evidence, psychological or other,
being offered in its behalf.

One indication of the pervasive influence of this psychoanalytic
paradigm is in an area of great concern to clinical psychology, the
classification of mental disorders. Thus the first two editions of the
American Psychiatric Association's *Diagnostic and Statistical Manual
of Mental Disorders* were based solidly on the "hydraulic paradigm"
of psychoneurosis.[14] The anxiety which is supposed to be at the
root of neurosis is accordingly construed in these influential volumes as a kind of force which "may be directly felt and expressed"
or "may be unconsciously and automatically controlled by the

13. Sigmund Freud, *The Origins of Psychoanalysis: Letters to Wilhelm Fliess, Drafts
and Notes* (London: Imago, 1954), p. 359.

14. American Psychiatric Association, *Diagnostic and Statistical Manual of Mental
Disorders,* 2nd ed. (Washington, D.C.: 1968).

utilization of various psychological defense mechanisms.'' It is
''produced by supercharged repressed emotions,'' and if not controlled by ''any specific psychological defense mechanism,'' it will
express itself in a conscious ''anxiety reaction'' or ''anxiety state.''
On the other hand, in another kind of neurosis, the dissociative reaction, ''the repressed impulse giving rise to the anxiety may be
discharged by, or deflected into, various symptomatic expressions
such as depersonalization, dissociated personality, stupor, fugue,
amnesia, dream state, somnambulism, etc.'' In ''conversion re-
actions,'' however, the ''impulse causing the anxiety is 'con-
verted' into functional symptoms in organs or parts of the body.''
In ''phobic reaction,'' the anxiety ''becomes detached from a specific idea, object, or situation in the daily life and is displaced to
some symbolic idea or situation.'' Finally, ''psychophysiologic
autonomic and visceral disorders'' are said to ''represent the visceral expression of affect which may be thereby prevented from
being conscious. The symptoms are due to a chronic and exag-
gerated state of the normal or physiological expression of emotion,
with the feeling, or subjective part, repressed.''[15]

What these excerpts represent obviously is not a descriptive classification or taxonomy of mental disorders but an explanatory or
etiological theory, couched in the categories of energy exchange
and borrowing, somewhat capriciously, from the Freudian theory
of the symbolic unconscious.

Sixteen years later (in 1968), the American Psychiatric Association's Committee on Nomenclature and Statistics was still main-
taining: ''Anxiety is the chief characteristic of the neuroses. It may
be felt and expressed directly, or it may be controlled unconsciously and automatically by conversion, displacement and various other psychological mechanisms.''[16] So deeply engrained had
this energy exchange paradigm for the neuroses become that in
1980, when a new American Psychiatric Association Task Force
on Nomenclature and Statistics sought to get away from the
Freudian paradigm, its chairman felt it could do so only by aban-
doning the category of neurosis in the new *Diagnostic and Statistical
Manual.*[17]

15. Ibid., 1st ed. (1952), pp. 29–33.
16. Ibid., 2nd ed. (1968), p. 39.
17. Ibid., 3rd ed. (1980), pp. 9–10.

The problem of classifying mental disorders or psychological abnormalities is still a vexing one, and the failure of either psychiatry or clinical psychology to deal effectively with it is a great stumbling block to scientific progress in psychopathology. Until we develop a meaningful and methodologically reasonable system for classifying mental disorders, we are in the unenviable position, scientifically speaking, of literally not knowing what we are talking about.

The taxonomy of abnormality is a problem principally in descriptive psychology, but the Freudian dynamic-hydraulic etiological paradigm is an absolute impediment to the descriptive attitude or set. I suggest that what is needed as an antidote is a truly phenomenological approach, one that construes experience in the hermeneutic manner, allowing reality as given to speak for itself, and that searches always in direct experience for the deeper meaning and the interrelationships which are characteristic of the things themselves. The hermeneutic method follows closely Husserl's injunction to go back to the things themselves (*"Zu den Sachen Selbst"*) and Heidegger's warning to "let Being be" (*Seingelassenheit*), not forcing it into any pre-fabricated paradigms, but allowing it to speak for itself. Hermeneutics is a method of *uncovering* (*unverborgen*), of remaining *with* the experience until it reveals its hidden inner truth (*aletheia*).

Behavioristic Reductionism

In sharp contrast with the hermeneutic method is the behavioristic reliance on the external paradigm, and how different are the consequences for psychology! Let us consider some of these consequences in an area of primary interest to the behaviorist, the experimental study of learning. Though behaviorism regards itself as maximally empirical in orientation, we have already noted that it accords self-evidence to only one aspect of experience, that of externally observable activity, or behavior. All other experiential data, such as the understanding of meanings, commitment to certain values, and the striving toward consciously formulated goals, are dismissed as at best irrelevant to the scientific understanding of human activity. In its most recent and most aggressive form the behaviorist paradigm insists that human behavior is exclusively determined by environmental contingencies of reinforcement which can be defined without reference to human awareness. The behaviorist method is thus diametrically opposed to the phenomenological or hermeneutic method. Basic to hermeneutics is the requirement that we attend to the whole of human experience, sequentially if not simultaneously, and the understanding that it is always illegitimate to neglect or "explain away" any possibly relevant *given* because of some contravening metaphysical or methodological assumption, e.g., to ignore conscious purpose in human action because environmental reinforcers are easier to identify and evaluate scientifically than are purposes, or because the understanding of one's own motivation is so vague and subjective. Thus to exclude from consideration conscious determinants and admit only behavioral ones is to beg the question and to offer evaluation without examination. It is to "explain" only by that which the method adopted permits you to study, viz., the externally observable, and this, in effect, denies the reality of what is given in experience in the first place, the consciously self-stated purpose. As Skinner's *Beyond Freedom and Dignity* has so clearly, if unwittingly, demonstrated, to ignore methodologically on principle is, in at least some instances, to deny ontologically what is self-evidently present.[18]

What are the consequences of focusing only on the readily measurable aspects of behavior, to the depreciatory neglect of cognitive aspects of the experienced situation? These can be seen with luminous clarity when we contemplate the strangely paralogical development of "classical conditioning" under behaviorist auspices. When Pavlov first noticed the salivation of dogs in response to activities or "stimuli" other than the placing of food powder on their tongues, he was convinced that he had discovered a "psychic reflex," a phenomenon for which the behaviorists, led by John Watson, much preferred the label "conditioned reflex" or "conditioned response." Watson and the many influenced by him saw the acquisition of conditioned responses as a model of simple learning, nicely amenable to experimental control and quantitative

18. Raymond J. McCall, "Beyond Reason and Evidence: The Metapsychology of Prof. B. F. Skinner," *Journal of Clinical Psychology* 28 (1972): 125–39.

assessment, and therefore a suitable basis for the development of a new behavioristic science of learning. Their enthusiastic faith has, over more than sixty years, generated thousands of studies of conditioning as the key to learning, studies characterized by a great deal of ingenuity and assiduity, yet leaving the questions of how we learn and how the process can be improved largely unanswered.

Even a cursory acquaintance with the vast literature of conditioning will convince the phenomenologically oriented that many learning specialists have been so beguiled by the behaviorist paradigm that they have ignored most of the most significant aspects of the learning experience. There has been a widespread tendency among behaviorists to overlook the fact that the "conditioned response" itself (for example, the dog's salivating in response to the ringing of a bell which has been associated with feeding) is only a small part of a total reaction, and this total reaction appears to be dominated not by the small amount of salivation involved but by the dog's cognition of the ringing bell as a signal of approaching food. Thus, quantitatively, the amount of salivation evoked by the bell is by no means as great as when food is actually placed on the dog's tongue. From a phenomenological perspective we must note that the dog does not chew and swallow as when food is in his mouth, and that the dog's posture is one of expectancy or anticipation, not consummation, as it is with food. If, moreover, the dog's expectation is dashed by the repeated failure of the bell ringer to feed him, the animal's anticipatory posture and his salivation alike will cease. To describe this entire process without any reference to the dog's cognizance of the connection between ringing bell and feeding is certainly to render an inadequate account of the event. Just because we have no direct experience of the dog's awareness is little reason for us to act as though the dog were *un*aware, and we can do so only by an elaborate pretense. From the behaviorist's own behavior we can tell that he knows that the dog *hears*—a form of cognition—so why should he find it necessary to ignore or deny the obvious truth that the dog can *recognize* certain sounds as indicators or signals of other events, the appearance of which he then anticipates? It is certainly not the dog's behavior that requires this pretense, since his muscular tension, his turning of his head in the direction of the bell, the cocking of his ears, all fit in nicely with signal recognition; and the small amount of salivation may itself be regarded as preparatory or anticipatory. (Even a behaviorist might acknowledge that when a dog's mouth waters, he is getting reading to eat!)

The refusal to see classical conditioning as generally instancing signal recognition prevents the behaviorist from doing justice to the psychology of salivation, to say nothing of the psychology of learning, and this stunning neglect appears to be dictated entirely by the biases inherent in the behavorist paradigm and its methodological implications. Here, it seems to me, is a striking confirmation of the hermeneutic principle that excluding certain items of immediate experience from the description of the situation being studied tends to distort the reality therein and renders at least doubtful any further analysis of that situation, no matter how well controlled or precisely measured it may be.

Further confirmation of this principle is evident in the destructive effects of this paradigmatic contamination of original data on the behavioristically inspired treatment of what is called "extinction of a conditioned response." The procedure, to be sure, is familiar and simple, though some of its implications are easily ignored or misunderstood. Let us suppose that we have established a conditioned response to the sound of a bell. If we repeatedly offer the conditioned stimulus (the sound of the bell) without the unconditioned stimulus (the feeding), the amount of saliva secreted gradually decreases until, after a goodly number of ringings without feeding, the animal ceases to salivate at the sound of the bell. Now since the conditioned response has ceased, says the behaviorist, we can say the learned response has been "extinguished," and we can no longer say that learning is taking place. Not all would say that the response has been *un*learned, but most would argue that the evidence for learning is no more. The phenomenologist, with his hermeneutic appreciation of the total situation, must regard this opinion as utterly ridiculous. "Extinction' is not a cessation of learning or an "unlearning" (whatever that may be), but a clear instance of *new learning*. And what is learned? That the previously noted connection between the conditioned stimulus and the unconditioned stimulus, the bell and the feeding, cannot anymore be counted on, that the bell is no longer a signal or a salient indicator of food in prospect; and this recognition of a change in the situation is as much a valid piece of information as was the earlier recognition of its utility as a signal. Viewing "extinction" as nonlearning is a manifestation of functional blindness, resulting from failure to look at the whole situation, focusing instead on one single aspect of it, salivation or non-salivation.

The behaviorist bias also produces a paradigm-determined presbyopia respecting the phenomenon labeled "stimulus generalization." Suppose that a dog has been conditioned to salivate at the sound of a bell and, when this relation is established, we substitute a buzzer for the bell. We note that the animal still salivates in response to the auditory signal, though not as much to the buzzer as to the bell. The salivation response, argues the behaviorist, has become attached to another new stimulus, or the learned response has become generalized. This, we are told, instances "learning by generalization." Preposterous! the phenomenologist would say. This kind of "generalization" is not learning at all, but simply failure to learn! The animal fails to discriminate adequately between a bell and a buzzer, which certainly is not to learn anything. If, however, we continue the experiment and repeatedly pair bell and food but not buzzer and food, the animal *will* learn the important fact that the bell is a signal for food but the buzzer is not. He will learn to discriminate, as all would agree. But to respond to the buzzer as well as to the bell is not-to-learn-to-discriminate, a special case of not-learning. One could, I suspect, read widely in the literature of learning without being given a hint that "extinction" is an example of learning and "generalization" is not. Yet, hermeneutically speaking, these are the facts revealed by the behaviorist's own data, when we pay attention to all the data.

There are many other respects in which behaviorist ontology has created a methodological prepossession leading us away from facts or data crucial to the understanding of the learning process. Thus behaviorist reductionism has led many psychologists to concentrate on elementary associative learning, such as the conditioning found in the simplest species of animals, to the neglect of the more nearly human modes of learning such as social imitative learning,[19] perceptual insight learning,[20] and conceptual learning.[21] We would scarcely suspect the presence in human beings of conceptual insight learning on a sustained and complex level if we confined ourselves to the behavioristically inspired literature. Thus the ratiocinative learning involved in mastering analytic geometry or logic or any advanced intellectual discipline has little or no place in the behaviorist scheme of things. One wonders indeed how it is possible with only the rudimentary cognitive equipment acknowledged by behaviorists to master the subtleties and refinements of behaviorism. Perhaps the answer is that it is not.

In their substantive view of the nature of human existence, we have seen that Boss and Heidegger reject the Cartesian separation of the mind as thinking things (*res cogitans*) from the extended reality (*res extensa*) of the world. In their view, human being present (*Dasein*) is not cut off from the world but is being present in the world and to the world (*in-der-Welt-sein*); and the greatest part of that world is made up of other human beings whom we *exist with* (*Mitsein*). Least of all, then, does the human being exist in isolation from his fellow man. While never questioning the ultimate individuality of each human existent, Boss would have little difficulty in conceding to Harry Stack Sullivan that personality is that which "manifests itself in interpersonal relations."[22] Boss would even add: We do not *have* relations with others; we *are* these relations. Thus:

> The fact that human existence is in every case "my" existence does not exclude "being with (*Mitsein*) others of my own kind. On the contrary, it is of the essence of *Dasein* to "be with." The "world" of man's being-in-the-world is ever and primordially one which I share

19. Albert Bandura and Richard H. Walters, *Social Learning and Personality Development* (New York: Holt, 1963).

20. Wolfgang Köhler, *The Mentality of Apes* (New York: Harcourt Brace, 1925).

21. Humphrey, *Thinking*, pp. 55 ff., 150 ff.; Wertheimer, *Productive Thinking*, pp. 69 ff.

22. Rychlak, *Personality and Psychotherapy*.

with others. The world of *Dasein* is essentially *Mitwelt.* For we never exist primarily as different subjects who only secondarily enter into interpersonal relations with one another and exchange ideas about the objects all of us perceive. Instead, as any direct observation shows, we are all out there in the world together, primarily and from the beginning. . . .[23]

As noted earlier, Sullivan and the Chicago school of sociology (Cooley, Mead, Sapir, et al.) that influenced him placed much stress on the complete dependence of the developing human on group attitudes and the evaluations of "significant others." To them it was nonsense to argue that we exist as human beings and then become socialized; rather, our humanity *is* our socialization since our very identity arises out of the perceptions others have of us. Even our self-concept is composed essentially of "the reflected appraisals of significant others." The Heidegger-Boss view, we have seen, is not as far from that position as one might imagine. According to that view, neither man's original nature nor his actual situation is of his own doing. He is "thrown" (*geworfen*) into a world he did not make, a world made up most importantly of other people and the things people have to make use of if they are to survive and thrive (the *Zuhandene*). By reason of his overwhelming dependence, man is caught up in (*verfallen*) the attitudes and values of the Other or the They (*das Man*), so that when we ask "What is man?" the answer is: "As others want and make him to be." This is Heidegger's *Man-selbst,* which has more than a passing resemblance to Fromm's "other-directed man" or Riesman's "radar man." Like Fromm, however, Boss and Heidegger insist that there is an element not merely of independence but of transcendence in man as we experience him. The human being can not only recognize the fulfillment of his own possibilities as his proper goal, but he can take steps to free himself from enslavement to the Other and move toward his own authenticity (*Eigentlichkeit*), a position that takes the human being well beyond Sullivanian "security" and "euphoria" and into *personhood,* a deepened version of Erich Fromm's notion of "man for himself."

23. Boss, *Psychoanalysis,* p. 55.

Phenomenology and the Paradigm
of Organismic Knowing

I have so far focused attention on continental European, mostly German-speaking, thinkers; but the possibility cannot be overlooked that we already have a home-grown hermeneutics in the self-theory of Carl Rogers. It seems very clear that Rogers is experientially oriented and holistically humanistic in his approach to human beings. Moreover, Rogers does explicitly identify his position with what he loosely categorizes as the "phenomenological, existential, self-theory, self-actualization stream of thought."[24] We need not plunge very deeply into this stream of thought, however, to realize that it owes little to European sources; indeed, one finds in Rogers's writings no reference to Boss, Binswanger, Heidegger, Husserl, or any other European phenomenologist or existentialist. Although Rogers does include American "phenomenologists" like Snygg and Combs and American "existentialists" like Maslow in the bibliography attached to his essay "Toward a Science of the Human Person," he seems to make little or no use of their very modest formulations of an existential or phenomenological nature, but relies instead on a highly generalized analysis of the "inward flow of experience" as identified in the interpersonal exchange with which he is most familiar, that of the psychotherapeutic relationship. Strangely, perhaps, this brief essay in the Wann volume is Rogers's only systematic treatment of the nature of human knowledge.

Curiously, however, his generalized analysis begins with an epistemological excursion into the nature of human knowledge. The most fundamental of his statements seems to be the proposition that all knowing consists essentially of hypotheses which we check in different ways, depending on which of three kinds of knowing is involved. The three kinds of knowing he classifies as subjective, objective, and interpersonal.

In subjective knowing we are dealing, says Rogers, with our own mental states, and even though I "know" that I love or hate,

---

24. Carl Rogers, "Toward a Science of the Human Person," in *Behaviorism and Phenomenology: Contrasting Bases for Modern Psychology*, ed. T. W. Wann (Chicago: University of Chicago Press, 1964), pp. 109–32.

believe or disbelieve, these are all only hypotheses to begin with.
Thus I may check such a hypothesis by asking, "Do I really hate
him?" and I may find that what I first thought was hate was really
envy. When asked, similarly, if I see a spot of light in a dark room,
I form an inner hypothesis that it is moving. These inner hypotheses are to be checked by referring to our inward flow of experiencing. This, says Rogers, seems to be our most basic way of
knowing, a deeply rooted organismic sensing, from which we form
and differentiate our conscious symbolizations and conceptions.

The logical and experiential coherence of this complex position
is far from evident. In the first place, the notion that *all* knowing
consists of hypotheses does not quite make sense, since we would
then not know anything directly and there would be no basis for
our hypotheses. This way of putting it may be simply a slip, because Rogers does acknowledge that our "inward flow of experiencing" is "our most basic way of knowing" and he would certainly regard this as direct knowing. In his view, however, it is a
subjective kind of knowing, so it tells us nothing about things outside ourselves. Through it I can decide, for example, whether my
feeling for another individual is hate or envy. Under the same
heading of "subjective knowing" Rogers also mentions as hypothetical the experience of a spot of light in a dark room as moving.
In his own words: "I form an inner hypothesis that it is moving."
As Wertheimer pointed out, however—and fairly rigorously demonstrated—motion, real or apparent, is directly perceived. Even if
the spot of light is actually stationary—as it is in the autokinetic
experiment, to which Rogers is apparently referring—it is still *perceived* as moving, and no checking with the "inward flow of our
experiencing" is going to alter that. More fundamentally, it is
dangerous to regard the perception of a spot of light, whether
moving or at rest, as entirely subjective. The subjectivity of perception is an epistemological assumption of a large order, on which
experimental investigations of illusions cast little light one way or
the other, though they do indicate that in the autokinetic phenomenon my perception of the light as moving is direct and clear;
it is the interpretation of this experienced movement, like that of
the sun around the earth, that remains to be clarified.

More in keeping with the phenomenological perspective is the notion of "hypotheses" regarding the nature of my own inner feeling, though the term "hypothesis" does not seem to be an entirely appropriate one to describe the phenomenon. Thus when I say to myself "I hate that man" there is nothing hypothetical about the fact of my feeling or its generally negative quality. What remains to be determined is the articulated structure of this negative feeling and its connection with other experiences. When by checking my experience more carefully I find that this negative feeling is tinctured with resentment for certain advantages this man may have over me, I realize that it is not just dislike I feel for him, but envy. What is needed to clarify my feeling is precisely the "uncovering" (*unverborgen*) that bespeaks the hermeneutic method. We penetrate more deeply into the experience in order to make explicit and clear certain aspects of it that are originally vague or murky. The original experience of "hatred," however, is implicit or unarticulated rather than hypothetical, while the final experience seems to be clearly conscious and in great part rational rather than based on some kind of semi-unconscious organismic sensing.

The second kind of knowing in Rogers's analysis, objective knowing, is also to him hypothetical in nature, but it is checked both by "externally observable operations" and by "empathic inference regarding the reactions of a trusted reference group," presumably the group of fellow scientific observers. This psychological process, in any case, is the basis of "all logical positivism, operationalism, and the vast structure of science as we know it."

In these contentions, Rogers parts company entirely with phenomenology. The notion that "empathic inferences regarding the reactions of a trusted reference group" have a large role to play in empirical observations seems highly questionable, since these observations are public and the processes of mathematical statement and analysis, to which the observed data are subjected, are based on consensually accepted principles. Moreover, while this procedure is the basis of much scientific activity, it is not the basis of logical positivism and operationalism. Logical positivism and operationalism are not scientific generalizations and do not make up any part of the "structure of science." They are, instead, highly speculative philosophical positions, resting not on particular observations or mathematical analyses but on logical and epistemological considerations, having to do with the nature of scientific inquiry and the desirability of extending procedures inspired by physical science to other types and subjects of investigation. It seems that Rogers's conception of scientific method is weakened by a confusion between scientific generalizations and principles, on the one hand, and, on the other, the now highly questionable extrapolations and evaluative pontifications of the logical positivists and the operationists who are, at best, philosophers of science and all too often propagandists of scientism. One might hope that Rogers would be acceptant of the anti-positivism of Michael Polanyi, for whom he expresses great admiration.

The third kind of knowing Rogers calls "interpersonal" or "phenomenological." "Here," he says, "I 'know' that you feel hurt by my remark or that you despise yourself . . ." Such conclusions, he contends, are also hypotheses, in this case checked by using empathic understanding in order "to get at the relative aspects of your phenomenal field, to get inside your private world of meanings." I may question you regarding this or I may create a climate which makes it safe for you to reveal your internal frame of reference.

It is evident that Rogers here is referring to the process of deriving information indirectly about your mental state from your words or by inference from nonverbal or other unintentional cues. It is certainly strange to call this kind of knowledge (or surmise) "phenomenological," since what is in question depends not only on experience but on faith in someone's word, or inference as to the validity of certain other indirect signs of mental state (which Rogers calls "empathic inference"). One might wonder also if "empathic inference" belongs in the same category of knowledge with direct awareness of one's own mental state or with empirical observation of the scientific type.

Even if we acknowledged that there are these three kinds of knowing, we would have to recognize that all together they would represent only a small fragment of the field of cognitive experience. Rogers's first kind of knowledge arises from the reflective probing of emotionally toned or subjectively denoted inner states; his second type from the intersubjective verification of the externally observable; and his third type either from belief in the word of another, or from empathic inference regarding another's feeling state. But no mention is made of knowledge derived from logical inference, deductive or inductive, based either on scientific or common-sense data or on the convergence of clinical indicators. What about knowledge based on mathematical or logical analysis of postulates or other propositions (the kind exemplified by Einstein in developing his theory of special relativity)? What about the aha! experience in creative thinking or problem solving, or in the intuition of esthetic meaning? All of these are certainly modes of knowing given in immediate experience, and their absence from Rogers's taxonomy of knowledge must be viewed by phenomenological psychologists as a telling weakness.

The Psychophysical Paralogism and the Psych-Illogical Paradigm

In contrast to the behaviorists and the orthodox psychoanalysts, contemporary neuropsychologists look for the key to human psychological functioning in the anatomical and physiological organization of the nervous system, particularly within and between the two hemispheres of the human forebrain. The general dependence of psychic activity (sensory perception, biological motivation, imagination, memory, conceptualization both verbal and nonverbal) on the two major portions of the forebrain, the *telencephalon* (which includes the cerebral cortex) and the *diencephalon* (which includes the hypothalamus), has been well documented by experimental and clinico-pathological studies. From these we know of the reliance of many of these functions on specific aspects of the cerebral system, e.g., of verbal conceptualization on the fronto-temporal regions of the left cerebral hemisphere and on the integration of functions between the two hemispheres. As the knowledge of these specific dependencies increases, so apparently does the temptation to *identify* the psychic function with its neural substrate. This is a form of *reductionism,* an ancient device for simplifying the understanding of psychological process.

Writing in the 1650s, long before the beginnings of neurological science, Thomas Hobbes offered the most classic simplicistic reduction of psychic activities to physical processes going on inside the head. Perception for Hobbes is nothing but motion in the head, caused by motion in some external object impinging on our senses. As much may be said for imagination and memory, though here the motion imparted to "some internal substance in the head" is weaker and less lively than is the motion of perception. Further, motion in the head, depending on whether it helps or hinders the "vital motion" around the heart, is what constitutes pleasure and pain. In Hobbes's own words, if the motion in the head "helpeth" the vital motion, ". . . it is called delight, contentment, or pleasure, which is nothing but motion in the head . . . and the same delight with reference to the object is called love, but when such motion weakeneth or hindereth the vital motion, then it is called pain; and in relation to that which causeth it, hatred."[25]

It would seem that for Hobbes there is no psychological reality other than motion: sense perception, imagination, pain and pleasure, desire and aversion, love and hate, are all motion. But the phenomenologist must note that Hobbes does not claim that any of these conditions or processes is experienced as motion, nor does he offer any evidence for identifying any of them with motion. In a sterling example of demonstration by declaration, Hobbes simply proclaims them to be "nothing but" (the hallmark phrase of reductionism) motion. The phenomenologist must also note that the *experience* of these various conditions, such as pleasure, desire, imagination, precedes their being equated with some kind of motion. The existence of such conditions is then something that is immediately given—as Locke saw clearly—by reflection on our own purely psychological experience.

By its very extremity, Hobbes's position highlights the insoluble dilemma of every reductionistic theory of psychological functioning. This is that the psychological experience is given and accepted by the reductionist prior to his identifying it with something else (something simpler, more clearly physical or behavioral or neurological or what have you). If the effect of the reduction (or identification with the simpler) is to deny or even to discount the validity of the original experience as known by *reflection*—Locke's term

---

25. Thomas Hobbes, *Leviathan* (1651), Part 1, "De Homine," in *The English Works of Thomas Hobbes,* vol. 4, ed. W. Molesworth (London: John Bone, 1840).

here is better, I think, than Titchener's *introspection*—then the reductionist is in the unenviable position of denying what he or she
had to assume in order to make the denial. This is not a question of
clarification or specification of what is originally lacking in clarity
or specificity—that is precisely what the hermeneutic method in-
vites us to do—but the discounting or negation of the psychological
(the cognitive or appetitive) as experienced. It is this that is self-
refuting. Clearly there is a certain irreducibility of the psychological as given in experience, which no physical or metaphysical or
methodological theory can legitimately gainsay.

When, then, the neuropsychologist identifies the psychological
function with the activity of the neural area involved, he is making
a metaphysical identification whose rationale is seldom or never
discussed and which is, therefore, just as supposititious as
Hobbes's equation of cognition and appetition with physical motion. The procedure is also, I fear, just as full of contradictions and
outlandish hypostatizations. Let me cite some examples from a recent, in many respects fascinating, book on the "split brain" and
interhemispheric integration.[26]

The authors, Gazzaniga and Le Doux, repeatedly attribute to
portions of the brain activities which are clearly psychic in character such as awareness of sense data, recognizing the solution to a
problem, understanding simple spoken words, pattern discrimination, and awareness of other knowledge possessed. Dualistic phi-
losophies would ascribe such activities to the mind or *psyche* as an
aspect of the human being distinct from, though possibly quite dependent on, brain activity. From a phenomenological point of
view, to be sure, the autonomous mind theory is as gratuitous as
the part-brain theory. Both go far beyond what the phenomenologist would say is given in experience, viz., that the human being
as a unit feels and thinks, understands, desires, and despairs.
Empirically derived neurological information shows unmistakably
the dependence of such psychic functions on neural anatomy and
physiology, but such information does not negate the psychic activity itself; on the contrary, it presupposes it as an experientially

26. Michael S. Gazzaniga and Joseph Le Doux, *The Integrated Mind* (New
York: Plenum, 1978).

identifiable state or act to be correlated—not identified—with these neurological parameters. But according to Gazzaniga and Le Doux, "One of the immediate and compelling consequences of brain bisection was that the interhemispheric exchange of information was totally disrupted, so that visual, tactual, proprioceptive, auditory and olfactory information presented to one hemisphere could be processed and dealt with in that half-brain, but these activities would go on *outside the realm of awareness of the other half-cerebrum.*"[27] Similarly, they indicate that when a written word was flashed to the right hemisphere of a bisected brain, ". . . the talking (left) hemisphere did not know. It did not see the picture. . . . Yet, clearly the right half-brain knew the answer, because it reacted appropriately to the correct stimulus."[28] Gazzaniga and Le Doux also speak of "a certain ignorance each hemisphere has of what is going on in the other."[29] Moreover: "The data suggested that while the right hemisphere does understand simple spoken words, it must gain meaning from the whole sound of the word and not from its phonemic elements."[30] They also note that: "A pattern discrimination was taught to one hemisphere."[31]

We are further told that "unilateral hypothalamic lesions produce striking differences in the eating rates of the two hemispheres of split monkeys."[32] So it would seem that hemispheres not only perceive and gain meaning; they also *eat!* But there is more: "The verbal system, while having nonverbal associations, could also become aware of knowledge possessed by one of the nonverbal systems by observing emitted behavior, which is to say, stored information."[33] Here it is unequivocally stated that one portion of the brain can use inference from observed behavior to arrive at a knowledge of the knowledge of a nonverbal system, which seems to rival the accomplishment of T. S. Eliot's mystical cat who was enraptured with the thought of the thought of the thought of his

27. Ibid., p. 3. Emphasis mine.
28. Ibid., p. 4.
29. Ibid., p. 83.
30. Ibid., p. 85.
31. Ibid., p. 125.
32. Ibid., p. 127.
33. Ibid., p. 136.

name.[34] We are also assured that "mental properties are real and
. . . they can exert control over the individual neural elements that
upon interaction give rise to mental phenomena."[35] In summary:

> These observations suggested to us that the right hemisphere in
> P. S. possesses qualities that are deserving of conscious status. His
> right hemisphere has a sense of self, for it knows the name it collec-
> tively shares with the left. It has feelings, for it can describe its mood.
> It has a sense of who it likes and what it likes, for it can name its
> favorite people and its favorite hobby. The right hemisphere in P. S.
> also has a sense of the future, for it knows what day tomorrow is.
> Furthermore, it has goals and aspirations for the future, for it can
> name its occupational choice.[36]

This right hemisphere has everything, it would seem, with the exception of good grammar, sex, and religion, and it is undoubtedly
working on these. In any event, we may conclude that "clearly in
the split-brain case . . . the phenomenon of one mental system's
watching another and, as a result, altering its behavior is explicitly
present."[37] These considerations lead the authors to remark that
split-brain studies have important implications regarding "free
will" and "the nature of personal responsibility." Thus: "Most of
our social institutions are built on the notion that man is personally
responsible for his actions, and implicit in that statement is a notion that man has a unitary nature embodied in the self. What are
we now to do with that view, given the possibility that *multiple selves
exist,* each of which can control behavior at various moments in
time?"[38]

The notion that these multiple activities are actually carried out
by these sections of the brain—despite the ridiculous and, strictly
speaking, contradictory conclusions to which this assumption leads
—is never questioned by the authors. Now what is actually given
in experience, as noted above, is simply that certain activities are

---

34. See T. S. Eliot, "The Naming of Cats," *Old Possum's Book of Practical Cats*
(New York: Harcourt, Brace & Co., 1939), p. 10.

35. Gazzaniga and Le Doux, *Integrated Mind,* p. 141.

36. Ibid., pp. 143–44.

37. Ibid., p. 157.

38. Ibid., p. 159. Emphasis mine.

performed by the damaged organism, activities that are cognitive or motivational and thus psychological, even though some neural elements, ordinarily involved as substrates of these activities, are in these instances missing. Because of the injury to the nervous system, the activities are likely to appear as altered and in some ways degraded; nevertheless, these acts are psychologically adaptive and enable the organism to register the situation in which it is placed and to behave appropriately and to some considerable degree effectively, even though a significant portion of its brain is out of action. This tells us something very important about brain function and its relation to the organism's capacity for psychological adaptation. But to contend that the psychologically adaptive activity is as such performed by a part of the brain is to commit the fallacy of confusing instrument with agent, which may be abetted by a half-conscious metaphysical assumption of a materialistic or physicalistic nature. Much of this kind of confusion would be mitigated by the simple device of employing an appropriate term to describe the relation between a given activity of an organism, on the one hand, and the neural mechanism by means of which the organism—not the mechanism—performs this activity, on the other. I suggest that the appropriate term for this purpose is the verb "mediate." It is thus correct to say "The eye mediates seeing" rather than "The eye sees," since it is *we* who see by means of our eyes. Even more incorrect than "The eye sees" is to say "The temporal lobes hear" or "The occipital lobes see" or "The hypothalamus experiences emotion," since in these cases the neural apparatus is only part of the sensory or motor mechanism. So, notwithstanding the claims of Gazzaniga and Le Doux, we do not speak with our left hemisphere, though our speech is mediated thereby, as well as by our larynx and various accessory structures. Phenomenologically, it is always the whole organism, taken as a unit, which sees, hears, thinks, and experiences motivation and emotion.

No one today would take seriously Hobbes's contention that "pleasure is nothing but motion in the head," but the reference to the "split-brain case" as involving "the phenomenon of one mental system's watching another and, as a result, altering its behavior,'' or the statement that ''unilateral hypothalamic lesions produce striking differences in the eating rates of the two hemispheres,'' represents very little conceptual advance despite the nearly 350 years of technological progress intervening.

The phenomenologist would further insist that activities or states that are essentially psychological are correctly describable only in psychological categories. The widespread tendency to ignore this principle and to ascribe to neural structures of one sort or another such activities as perceiving, feeling, understanding, intending, and reflecting is a disposition that needs to be labeled. Since it involves a fallacy or *paralogism* which rests in great part on a confusion of the psychological and the physiological, an appropriate name for it would be the psychophysical paralogism.'' The paradigm on which this fallacy is based would seem to be one that obscures or fudges the distinction between the psychological state or activity and the neurophysiological conditions that mediate it, even though the psychological state is initially accepted as experienced and the neurophysiological conditions are *not* as such experienced. This, then, is not truly a physicalistic model but a confused or contradictory semi-psychological, quasi physiological paradigm which, in a doubtful venture into punning, I have called the ''psych-illogical paradigm,'' or the ''psych-illogical model.''

If the typical attitude of our contemporaries toward the essential nature of psychological functioning is not a physicalistic one, neither can it be described as a ''psychophysical parallelism,'' a consistent, if not very satisfying, conception; nor can this attitude be described as one that shows a proper appreciation of the psychic as such. It seems to rest on a fallacy of maximum incognizance, a simple failure to realize that the psychic cannot be described in physical terms. The attitude is so characterized by ambivalence, ambiguity, and inconsistency that I am tempted to label it ''split mind,'' leaving the ''split-brain'' to Gazzaniga and Le Doux. Since, however, the term ''split-mind'' has already been preempted by amateur psychopathologists, especially editorial writers, I will hesitantly refer to the currently popular model as the ''psych-illogical paradigm.'' It is close to the very antithesis of the hermeneutically open approach of Heidegger to experience, almost a hermetically sealed approach like that of the behaviorists, one that experience will never pry open.

Summary

I have advanced the concept of phenomenological psychology as a pre-science whose emergence heralds the possibility of a fundamental change in psychology as an empirical discipline. That some such change is in order is illustrated by the long-standing failure of the leading systems of psychological theory and methodology (chiefly psychoanalysis and behaviorism) to provide a satisfactory empirical explanation of such phenomena as human learning, motivation, intellectual and moral development, and the classification and rectification of human abnormality.

In striving to achieve for psychology the status of a science, many psychologists have modeled their discipline closely on the physical sciences and have attempted to consolidate their position by treating psychological questions by methods borrowed from the natural sciences such as the hypotheticodeductive method. They have also made some use of the related notion of scientific paradigm, borrowed largely from Thomas Kuhn's *The Structure of Scientific Revolutions,* as a technical conception for investing their theories and methods with scientific character.

It is by no means certain, however, that Kuhn's rather vague conception of paradigm can do much to further psychology's scientific ambitions. When this "paradigm" is seen to be very similar to the hypothesis portion of the hypotheticodeductive method as exemplified in the evolution of the physical sciences, just how little utility it has for psychology becomes clear. To begin with, the hypotheticodeductive method requires well-established inductive generalizations as a foundation for its deductive and verification procedures, and psychology has arrived at no such inductive universals. What psychology has had to be satisfied with, instead, is sampling methods (as a substitute for the "sufficient enumeration" of inductive reasoning) and tendential generalizations of the collective type (as a substitute for divisive or authentic universals). Psychology thus cannot *deduce* in the strict sense but only *extrapolate,* though it may perform the latter operation both carefully and critically.

Psychoanalytic physicalism showed its debt to the mechanistic approach of Helmholtzian physics at first by striving to imitate it (as in Freud's *Project for a Scientific Psychology*), then, when this proved unworkable, by adopting a model of explanation ("psychic energy") that amounted to a crude analogizing of a purely physical model. Freud's greatest interest was in explaining human motivation, and Freudian psychodynamics construes this motivation almost entirely in the categories of energy exchange and transformation. The ceaseless quest for pleasure and the avoidance of pain is the *Lustprinzip* which lies at the root of all human motives. But pain is associated with the buildup of energy in the psychic system and pleasure with the rapid release of energy. Even the Freudian conception of *libido* as the foundation of all, or almost all, human action is more of the same "energy economics," since libido is defined as the "psychic energy of the sex drive." None of these identifications has an iota of evidence in its support.

Although the attempt by Freudian psychiatry to build a classification scheme or taxonomy of neurotic disorders around the notion of psychic energy was a signal failure and has been abandoned in the most recent edition of the American Psychiatric Association's *Diagnostic and Statistical Manual,* the psychoanalytic system remains based on a kind of pre-fabricated paradigm, borrowed from nineteenth-century physics and imposed on human aberration. Even if this superimposition had been intended at first as merely a convenient analogical conceptualization, it has come to enter into psychoanalytic thinking in a quite literal fashion.

Behavioristic reductionism also depends on an extraneous paradigm, that of "behavior" or activity-as-observed-ab-extra, as the only kind of human activity worthy of investigation. Any experience not in keeping with this paradigm is ignored or explained away as irrelevant to scientific understanding or as simply deceptive. Behaviorism is thus diametrically opposed to the hermeneutic method of phenomenology. To the phenomenologist, behaviorism's total focus on behavior inevitably results in an ignoring of significant aspects of our experience, such as our awareness of what we are doing and our motivational inclinations. With no reference to cognition or motivation permitted, the psychological dimension of human life is gutted and the resulting description of human activity essentially trivial. Even the description of animal behavior is vitiated by the behaviorists' selective imperception. In simple conditioning of the Pavlovian type, for example, the behaviorist takes no account of the signal recognition essential to the entire process. Focusing on behavior, too, the behaviorist misses the element of learning in the process he calls "extinction," and misses the point that "stimulus generalization" is a failure to learn rather than a kind of learning. Preoccupied as they are with simple associative learning, behaviorists have little or nothing to tell us about distinctively human learning such as insight learning, conceptual learning, systematic ratiocinative learning, or the sociocultural learning so essential to the understanding of human development.

In contrast with both psychoanalysis and behaviorism, Daseinanalysis places primary emphasis on social learning and the socialization of human development. *Dasein* or Human Presence is *in* the world and not a Cartesian mind, boarded up in its own ideas and cut off from material (and social) entities. Boss seems at times close to Harry Stack Sullivan's position that human personality is defined by its interpersonal relations, though the views of Heidegger and Boss also allow for the individual's capacity to transcend the group and to move toward personal authenticity (*Eigentlichkeit*), a position closer, perhaps, to Erich Fromm than to Sullivan.

In Carl Rogers's combination of self-theory and phenomenology, the classification of the kinds of knowing seems confused as well as tendentious. The reliance on a principle of "organismic sensing" reads like a pure act of faith, neither paradigmatic nor hermeneutic in origin.

Finally, the technologically interesting developments in neuropsychology suffer from a paradigmatic confusion of the psychological and the physiological and an astonishing disposition to view morphological segments of the central nervous system as psychic agents in their own right. Between the "psych-illogical paradigm" and the "psychophysical paralogism," both Freud's "psychology for neurologists" and Gazzaniga and Le Doux's "neuroanatomy for psychologists" seem certain only to compound the confusion in our understanding of the relations between psychological experience and the morphology and physiology of the cerebrum.

Index

Ach, Narziss: study of practical decision-making, 43–44

Angel, Ernest, 82

Angst: as different from psychopathological anxiety, 78; distinction from anguish and dread, 78–79; relation to uncanniness (*Unheimlichkeit*), 79–80; indefiniteness of object, 80; as prelude to self-recognition, 80–81

Aquinas, St. Thomas, 11, 12, 36

Aristotelian-Thomistic tradition: its treatment of psyche or soul, 12; influence on Brentano, 36

Aristotle: mind as originally blank tablet, 17; analysis of association, 20

Association of ideas: in Aristotle related to directive thinking, 20; Hobbes's reduction to simple contiguity, 20–21; for James Mill purely passive reflection, 21

Augustine, St.: soul as radically different from body, 11

Augustinian-Platonic tradition: true home of soul in union with the divine, 12

Bandura, Albert: social imitative learning as distinctively human, 118

Befindlichkeit (situatedness): meaning of, 77; distinction from man's understanding (*Verstehen*) of his possibilities, 77–78

Behavioral methods: as independent of behavioristic assumptions, 108

Behaviorism: as a restrictive paradigm, 113–15; complete opposition to hermeneutic method, 114; neg-

lect of cognitive variables such as signal recognition, 115; expectancy, 115–16; failure to see extinction as learning, 116–17; or generalization as failure to learn, 117; neglect of distinctively human modes of learning, 118

Berkeley, George: denial that some ideas are more objective than others, 19; no justification for supposing that material substances exist, 19

Binet, Alfred: studies of intellectual function supportive of Würzburg school, 47

Binswanger, Ludwig: introduced Boss to Heidegger's ideas, 6; little influence on American psychology, 96

Bleuler, Eugen: influenced Boss, 5

Boss, Medard: applications and extensions of Heidegger's ideas, 3, 4, 7, 64, 65, 66, 72, 76; background in psychoanalysis, 5–6; relations with Heidegger, 6; attitude toward the empirical method in psychology, 6–8

Brentano, Franz: background in the Aristotelian-Thomistic tradition, 36; perception as act rather than content, 36; "intentional being" or "immanent objectivity" as characteristic of mental act, 36–37; inner perception as distinct from Wundtian introspection, 38–39

Bridgman, Percy: influence of his operationism on mid-twentieth century psychology, 102

Bühler, Karl: experimental study of difficult intellectual problems, 45–47

JACKET DESIGNED BY IRVING PERKINS ASSOCIATES
COMPOSED BY THE COMPOSING ROOM, KIMBERLY, WISCONSIN
MANUFACTURED BY MALLOY LITHOGRAPHING, INC., ANN ARBOR, MICHIGAN
TEXT AND DISPLAY LINES ARE SET IN BASKERVILLE

Library of Congress Cataloging in Publication Data
McCall, Raymond J. (Raymond Joseph), 1913–
Phenomenological psychology.
Includes bibliographical references and index.
1. Phenomenological psychology. 2. Heidegger, Martin,
1889–1976. I. Title.
BF204.5.M3 1983   150.19′2   83-47764
ISBN 0-299-09410-3
ISBN 0-299-09414-6 (pbk.)